DEDICATION

To the memory of the brave men of Hill's Corps, who were killed while fighting under the orders of General Longstreet, on the afternoon of July 3rd, 1863; whose fame has been clouded by the persistent misrepresentations of certain of their comrades, this "little book" is affectionately dedicated.

W. R. B.
Scotland Neck, Halifax Co., N. C,
October, 1888

PICKETT OR PETTIGREW?

AN

HISTORICAL ESSAY

[revised and enlarged.]

CAPTAIN W. R. BOND

Sometime Officer, Brigade Staff, Army of Northern Virginia

W. L. L. HALL. Publisher
Scotland Neck, N.C.

Foreword by Michael C. Hardy

Wake Forest, NC
www.scuppernongpress.com

Pickett or Pettigrew?
An Historical Essay
By Captain W. R. Bond
Foreword by Michael C. Hardy

©2019 The Scuppernong Press

First Printing

The Scuppernong Press
PO Box 1724
Wake Forest, NC 27588
www.scuppernongpress.com

Cover and book design by Frank B. Powell, III

All rights reserved. Printed in the United States of America.

No part of this book may be reproduced or transmitted in any form or by any means, electronic or mechanical, including photocopying, recording, or by any information and storage and retrieval system, without written permission from the editor and/or publisher.

International Standard Book Number ISBN 978-1-942806-20-2

Library of Congress Control Number: 2019944089

Contents

Introduction iii

Foreword v

Preface vii

General James Johnston Pettigrew ix

Pickett or Pettigrew? 1

Appendix 51

General George Edward Pickett 63

General Pickett

General Pettigrew

Introduction

Pickett or Pettigrew? This has been a question discussed since shortly after the end of the War for Southern Independence. Once the horrors of the so-called *reconstruction* of the former Confederate states was over and people of the South could resume a somewhat normal life they began to study the *late unpleasantness* and shared their stories so future generations would know what had transpired during those four long years of war and sacrifice.

North Carolinians in particular realized their story was not being told, or if told, was inaccurate. The third day of the Battle of Gettysburg was the most egregious.

Many of the officers of North Carolina troops were dead and could not tell their stories. Captain W. R. Bond, a veteran of the Army of Northern Virginia, set out to correct this omission in history with his pamphlet, *Pickett or Pettigrew? An Historical Essay,* first published in 1888.

Bond shows undue credit has been given to General Pickett and Virginia troops and gives examples to prove his claims. Mississippi and Tennessee troops have also been denied the proper credit due them and this is also pointed out with proof.

General Robert E. Lee once stated it was a shame the best generals in the Confederacy were in Richmond editing newspapers. It seems a lot of the misinformation about the Battle of Gettysburg was generated by the newspapers in Richmond.

This is a reprint of the second edition of Bond's work which includes letters and testimonies from readers, both North and South, which back up his findings which were included in the back. Only a very few typos were corrected. It has been completely reset in a modern typeface with photos of the two generals included in this edition along with a foreword by Michael Hardy.

The Scuppernong Press is proud to bring this pamphlet back into print for readers in the twenty-first century to learn and enjoy. We hope it will inspire our readers to explore further the events of July 3, 1863.

— *Frank B. Powell, III*
Editor

Foreword

In 1888, Capt. William R. Bond waded into a discussion which had raged since the evening of July 3, 1863: who was at fault for the failure that day as the Confederate forces charged the Federals posted on the slopes south of Gettysburg. It was the contention of many high-ranking Virginia officers that the "support troops," under the command of James J. Pettigrew and Isaac Trimble, had failed to support the Virginians under George Pickett. This move denied Confederate forces their chance for victory.

The idea spread from the grumbling of officers to the editorials of Virginia newspaper publishers. Since so many North Carolina officers and men were dead, wounded, or taken as prisoners following the battle, not many spoke out to right the wrongs being cast upon the character of Tar Heel soldiers. Following the war, much of the press was quiet on the matter. Men from many states were trying to rebuild their lives, homes, and communities. In 1877, Col. Walter Taylor, who had served on the staff of General Robert E. Lee, published his reminiscences, again asserting that Pickett spearheaded the attack, with Pettigrew and Trimble in support. This time, however, Tar Heels took up the battle. The *Raleigh Observer* sent a questionnaire to as many North Carolina officers as they could locate, asking about their involvement and what they had witnessed that hot July afternoon. The rebuttals to Taylor's assertions were printed on October 30, 1877.

Obviously, Bond was not satisfied. The newspaper columns were not widely available outside the state. The captain set out to craft his own refutation to the disparaging claims of Walter Taylor and so many others. However, instead of giving an account of what he had witnessed, Bond used what sources were available to him at the time, along with testimonials of Federal commanders. The end product was *Pickett or Pettigrew: An Historical Essay.*

Bond begins by looking at the life of James J. Pettigrew, the "most promising man of the South." He then lambasts Virginia writers and newspaper editors for discriminating against troops from other states. The greatest amount of time is spent on actual numbers, comparing the men lost by various North Carolina regiments, and by regiment from other Southern states, like Mississippi and Louisiana, to those lost by Virginia regiments and brigades, not only during the battle of Gettysburg, but also in other battles during the war.

Bond takes a deeper look into various North Carolina regiments and brigades, like those led by Thomas L. Clingman and William W. Kirkland, the Junior Reserves, and the heavy artillery batteries, that, up until the closing days of the conflict, had been on garrison duty at Forts Fisher and Caswell. The captain finishes the second edition with testimonials from people who had read his "pamphlet." Some of his reviewers were from the South, but many had fought against North Carolinians during the battle of Gettysburg. Positive reviews came from men who had seen their fair share of hard fighting, serving in regiments like the Fifth New Hampshire, Twelfth New Jersey, and Eighty-eighth Pennsylvania.

Those testimonials from former foes validated Bond's assertions. The Tar Heels and other troops from various states in the lines to the left of Pickett's men were not there to support the Virginians, but to extend the line. And in the end, these troops went further and lost more, sacrificed more, than the Virginians who get the credit in history.

This new, edited version of *Pickett or Pettigrew?* is a welcome addition to the world of North Carolina historiography. The North Carolina perspective on America's pivotal battle is often lacking, and this new, updated volume will help fill a much-needed gap in the story of those hot July days of 1863.

Michael C. Hardy
March 1, 2019

Preface

The first edition of this pamphlet appeared a short time before the publication of the *Official Records* relating to Gettysburg. Consequently many things of importance to the subject treated were unknown to the writer. Such facts as he possessed of his own knowledge or could gather from his comrades and other sources, together with a lot of statistics secured from the War Department, were published and with gratifying results. Very many of the statements then made and which were not open to successful contradiction were so much at variance with the general belief that the brochure attracted wide attention, especially among old soldiers. From Tacoma on the Pacific slope and Augusta, Maine, from Chicago and New Orleans, came assurances of interest and appreciation. In fact there are very few States from which there have not come expressions either of surprise that the slander should ever have originated or of sympathy with the effort to right a great wrong.

That the two thousand copies formerly issued should have been disposed of two years ago and that there is still a demand for the pamphlet, is deemed sufficient reason for this edition. And the recent publication in New York of a history repeating the old falsehoods emphasizes the need of keeping the facts before the public.

It would be a matter of regret should any statement in these pages wound the sensibilities of any personal friends of the author, still in such an event he would be measurably consoled by the reflection that here as in most matters it is best to "hew to the line and let the chips fall as they may."

Scotland Neck, N.C., April, 1900

General James Johnston Pettigrew

General James Johnston Pettigrew

*"There lived a knight, when knighthood was in flow'r,
Who charm'd alike the till-yard amd the bower."*

The family of Johnston Pettigrew was one of the oldest, wealthiest and most influential of Eastern Carolina. His grandfather, Rev. Chas. Pettigrew, was the first Bishop-elect of the Diocese of North Carolina. He was born upon his father's estate, Bonarva, Lake Scuppernong, Tyrrell County, North Carolina, on July 4th, 1828, and died near Bunker's Hill, Va., July 17th, 1863, having been wounded three days before in a skirmish at Falling Waters. He graduated with the first distinction at the University of North Carolina in 1847. A few months after graduation, at the request of Commodore Maury, principal of the Naval Observatory at Washington, he accepted a professorship in that institution. Having remained there about eight months he resigned and went to Charleston, South Carolina, and became a student of law, in the office of his distinguished relative, Hon. Jas. L. Pettigru, obtaining a license in 1849.

In 1850 he went to Europe to study the civil law in the German Universities. There also he became thoroughly acquainted with the German, French, Italian and Spanish languages. He became so well acquainted with Arabic as to read and appreciate it; also with Hebrew. He then traveled over the various countries of the Continent, also England, Scotland and Ireland. In 1852 he became Secretary of Legation to the U. S. Minister at the Court of Madrid. In the winter of 1861 he had printed in Charleston, for private circulation, an octavo volume of 430 pages, entitled *Spain and the Spaniards*, which has been very much admired by every one who has read it, for its learning, its research and the elegance of its style. Having remained in Madrid only a few months he returned to Charleston and entered upon the practice of law with Mr. James L. Pettigru. In December, 1856, and December, 1857, he was chosen a member of the Legislature from the city of Charleston. He rose to great distinction in that body, by his speech on the organization of the Supreme Court, and his report against the re-opening of the African Slave Trade. He failed to be re-elected in 1858. Again in 1859 he went to Europe with the intention of taking part in the war then in progress between Sardinia and

Austria. His application to Count Cavour for a position in the Sardinian Army, under General Marmora, was favorably received. His rank would have been at least that of colonel; but in consequence of the results of the battle of Solferino, which took place just before his arrival in Sardinia, the war was closed and he was thereby prevented from experiencing active military service and learning its lessons.

In 1859 he became colonel of a rifle regiment that was formed and that acted a conspicuous part around Charleston in the winter of 1860-61. With his regiment he took possession of Castle Pinkney, and was afterwards transferred to Morris Island, where he erected formidable batteries. He held himself in readiness to storm Fort Sumter in case it had not been surrendered after bombardment. In the spring of 1861, his regiment growing impatient because it could not just then be incorporated in the Confederate Army, disbanded; Colonel Pettigrew then joined Hampton's Legion as a private, and went with that body to Virginia, where active service was to be met with. A few days afterwards, without any solicitation on his part, he was elected colonel of the 22nd North Carolina Troops. While at Evansport, he was offered promotion, but declined it, upon the ground, that it would separate him from his regiment. Late in the spring of 1862 an arrangement was made by which his regiment was embraced in the brigade. He then accepted the commission. He and his brigade were with General Johnston at Yorktown and in the retreat up the peninsula. He was with his brigade in the sanguinary battle of Seven Pines, or Fair Oaks, where he was severely wounded, and left insensible upon the field and captured. He was in prison only about two months, and on being exchanged he returned to find that in his absence his beloved brigade had been given to General Pender. A new brigade was then made up for him. How well this body was disciplined and of what material it was made, this essay has attempted to show. In the autumn of 1862, he was ordered with his brigade to Eastern North Carolina, where he was engaged in several affairs, which though brilliant have been overshadowed by the greater battles of the war. In May, 1863, his brigade was again ordered to Virginia, and ever after formed a part of the Army of Northern Virginia. While commanding Heth's Division, in Longstreet's Assault, though his horse had been killed, and he had received a painful wound — a grapeshot shattering his left hand — he was within in a few feet of his own brigade when the final repulse came. On his regaining our lines, his remark to General Lee that he was responsible for his brigade, but not for the division, shows that he was satisfied with the conduct of a part, but not with that of all the troops under his command.

As to one of the two brigades that gave way before the rest of the line, he labored under a very great misapprehension. He did not know then, and the reading world has been slow to realize since, how very great had been its loss before retreating. As to the fact that in proportion to the number carried into the assault its loss had been more than twice as great as that of any of Pickett's brigades, there is not the slightest doubt. The highest praise and not censure should be its reward.

At Falling Waters, on the 14th, he had just been placed in command of the rear guard, which consisted of his own and Archer's brigade, when a skirmish occurred in which he was mortally wounded. He died on the 17th, and his remains were taken to his old home, Bonarva, and there he lies buried near the beautiful lake, whose sandy shores his youthful feet were wont to tread.

May he rest in peace!

Pickett or Pettigrew?

Longstreet's assault on the third day at Gettysburg, or what is generally, but very incorrectly, known as "Pickett's Charge," has not only had its proper place in books treating of the war, but has been more written about in newspapers and magazines than any event in American history. Some of these accounts are simply silly. Some are false in statement. Some are false in inference. All in some respects are untrue.

Three divisions, containing nine brigades and numbering about nine thousand and seven hundred officers and men, were selected for the assaulting column. The field over which they were ordered to march slowly and deliberately, was about one thousand yards wide, and was swept by the fire of one hundred cannon and twenty thousand muskets. The smoke from the preceding cannonade, which rested upon the field, was their only cover. In view of the fact, that when the order to go forward was given, Cemetery Ridge was not defended by Indians or Mexicans, but by an army, which for the greater part, was composed of native Americans, an army, which if it had never done so before, had shown in the first and second day's battles, not only that it could fight, but could fight desperately. In view of this fact, whether the order to go forward was a wise thing or a frightful blunder, I do not propose to discuss. The purpose of this paper will be to compare and contrast the courage, endurance and soldierly qualities of the different brigades engaged in this assault, dwelling especially upon the conduct of the troops commanded respectively by Generals Pickett and Pettigrew.

If certain heading facts are repeated at the risk of monotony, it will be for the purpose of impressing them upon the memories of youthful readers of history. As a sample, but rather an extreme one, of the thousand and one foolish things which have been written of this affair, I will state that a magazine for children, *St. Nicholas,* I think it was, some time ago contained a description of this assault, in which a comparison was drawn between the troops engaged, and language something like the following was used: "Those on the left faltered and fled. The right behaved gloriously. Each body acted according to its nature, for they were made of different stuff. The one of common earth, the other of finest clay. Pettigrew's men were North Carolinians, Pickett's were superb Virginians." To those people who do not know how the trash which passes for Southern history was manufactured, the motives which actuated the writers, and how greedily at first everything written by them about the war, was read, it is not so astonishing that a libel containing so much ignorance, narrowness and prejudice as the above should have been printed in a respectable publication, as the fact, that even to this day, when official records and other data are so accessible, there are thousands of otherwise well-informed people all over the land who believe the slander to be either entirely or in part true. And it looks almost like a hopeless task to attempt to combat an error which has lived so long and flourished so extensively. But some one has said, "Truth is a Krupp gun, before which falsehood's armor, however thick, cannot stand. One shot may accomplish nothing, or two, or three, but keep firing it will be pierced at last, and its builders and defenders will be covered with confusion." This little essay shall be my one shot, and may Justice It 'fend the right.

In the great war the soldiers from New York and North Carolina filled more graves than those from any of the other States. In the one case fourteen and in the other thirty-six percent of them died in supporting a cause which each side believed to be just.

Virginia, North Carolina and Georgia each had about the same number of infantry at Gettysburg, in all twenty-four brigades of the thirty-seven present. Now, this battle is not generally considered a North Carolina fight as is Chancellorsville, but even here the soldiers of the Old North State met with a greater loss (killed and wounded, remember, for North Carolina troops never attempted to rival certain Virginia brigades in the number of men captured), than did those from any other State, and, leaving out Georgians, greater than did those from any two States. Though the military population of North Carolina was exceeded by that of Virginia and Tennessee, she had, during the war, more men killed upon the battlefield than both of them together. This is a matter of record. It may be that she was a little deliberate in making up her mind to go to war, but when once she went in she went in to stay. At the close of the terrible struggle in which so much of her best blood had been shed, her soldiers surrendered at Appomattox and Greensboro more muskets than did those from any other State in the Confederacy. Why troops with this record should not now stand as high everywhere as they did years ago in Lee's and Johnston's armies, may appear a problem hard to solve, but its solution is the simplest thing in the world, and I will presently give it.

The crack brigades of General Lee's army were noted for their close fighting. When they entered a battle they went in to kill, and they knew that many of the enemy could not be killed at long range. This style of fighting was dangerous, and of course the necessary consequence in the shape of a casualty list, large either in numbers or percentage, followed. Then there were some troops in the army who would on all occasions blaze away and waste ammunition, satisfied if only they were making a noise. Had they belonged to the army of that Mexican general who styled himself the "Napoleon of the West," they would not have been selected for his "Old Guard," but yet, without exception, they stood high in the estimation of the Richmond people, much higher indeed than very many of the best troops in our army.

As said above, Longstreet's assault is almost invariably spoken and written of as "Pickett's Charge." This name and all the name implies, is what I shall protest against in this article. At the battle of Thermopylae three hundred Spartans and seven hundred Thespians sacrificed their lives for the good of Greece. Every one has praised Leonidas and his Spartans. How many have ever so much as heard of the equally brave Thespians? I do not know of a case other than this of the Thespians, where a gallant body of soldiers has been treated so cruelly by history, as the division which fought the first day under Heth and the third under Pettigrew. I have no personal concern in the fame of these troops, as I belonged to and fought in another division; but in two of its brigades I had intimate friends who were killed in this battle, and on their account I would like to see justice done.

Among these friends were Captain Tom Holliday, A.A.G., of Davis' Brigade, and Harry Burgwyn, Colonel of the 26th North Carolina. (This regiment had more men killed and wounded in this battle than any one of the seven hundred Confederate or the two thousand Federal ever had in any battle. Official records show this.) And then, too, I know of no reason why truth, honesty and fair dealing should not be as much prized in historical as in business matters.

As the battle of Gettysburg was the most sanguinary of the war, as by many it is considered "the turning of the tide," so the final charge made preceded and attended as it was by peculiarly dramatic circumstances, has furnished a subject for more speeches, historical essays, paintings and poems than any event which ever occurred in America. Painters and poets, whose subjects are historical, of course look to history for their authority. If history is false, falsehood will soon become intrenched in poetry and art.

The world at large gets its ideas of the late war from Northern sources. Northern historians, when the subject is peculiarly Southern, from such histories as Pollard's, Cook's and McCabe's, and these merely reflected the opinions of the Richmond newspapers. These newspapers in turn got their supposed facts from their army correspondents, and they were very careful to have only such correspondents as would write what their patrons cared most to read.

During the late war, Richmond, judged by its newspapers, was the most provincial town in the world. Though the capital city of a gallant young nation, and though the troops from every State thereof were shedding their blood in her defence, she was wonderfully narrow and selfish. While the citizens of Virginia were filling nearly one-half of the positions of honor and trust, civil and military, Richmond thought that all should be thus filled. With rare exceptions, no soldier, no sailor, no jurist, no statesman, who did not hail from their State was ever admired or spoken well of. No army but General Lee's and no troops in that army other than Virginians, unless they happened to be few in numbers, as was the case of the Louisianians and Texans, were ever praised. A skirmish in which a Virginian regiment or brigade was engaged was magnified into a fight, an action in which a few were killed was a severe battle, and if by chance they were called upon to bleed freely, then, according to the Richmond papers, troops from some other State were to blame for it, and no such appalling slaughter had ever been witnessed in the world's history.

Indiscriminate praise had a very demoralizing effect upon many of their troops. They were soon taught that they could save their skins and make a reputation, too, by being always provided with an able corps of correspondents. If they behaved well it was all right; if they did not it was equally all right, for their short-comings could be put upon other troops The favoritism displayed by several superior officers in General Lee's army was unbounded, and the wonder is that this army should have continued to the end in so high a state of efficiency. But then as the slaps and bangs of a harsh stepmother may have a less injurious effect upon the characters of some children than the excessive indulgence of a silly parent, so the morale of those troops, who were naturally steady and true, was less impaired by their being always pushed to the front when danger threatened, than if they had always been sheltered or held in reserve.

Naturally the world turned to the Richmond newspapers for Southern history, and with what results I will give an illustration: All war histories teach that in Longstreet's assault on the third day his right division (Pickett's) displayed more gallantry and shed more blood, in proportion to numbers engaged, than any other troops on any occasion ever had. Now, if gallantry can be measured by the number or percentage of deaths and wounds, and by the fortitude with which casualties are borne, then there were several commands engaged in this assault, which displayed more gallantry than any brigade in General Longstreet's pet division. Who is there who knows anything of this battle to whom the name of Virginia is not familiar?

To how many does the name of Gettysburg suggest the names of Tennessee, Mississippi or North Carolina? And yet the Tennessee brigade suffered severely: but the courage of its survivors was unimpaired. There were three Mississippi regiments in Davis' brigade, which between them had one hundred and forty-one men killed on the field. Pickett's dead numbered not quite fifteen to the regiment. The five North Carolina regiments of Pettigrew's Division bore with fortitude a loss of two hundred and twenty-nine killed.

Pickett's fifteen Virginia regiments were fearfully demoralized by a loss of two hundred and twenty-four killed. Virginia and North Carolina had each about the same number of infantry in this battle. The former had three hundred and seventy-five killed, the latter six hundred and ninety-six.

When in antebellum days, Governor Holden, the then leader of the Democratic cohorts in North Carolina, was the editor of the *Raleigh Standard*, he boasted that he could kill and make alive. The Richmond editors during the war combining local and intellectual advantages without boasting did the same. They had the same power over reputations that the Almighty has over physical matter. This fact General Longstreet soon learned, and the lesson once learned, he made the most of it. He would praise their pet troops and they would praise him, and between them everything was lovely. He was an able soldier, "an able writer, but an ungenerous." Troops from another corps, who might be temporarily assigned to him were invariably either ignored or slandered.

The Gascons have long been noted in history for their peculiarity of uniting great boastfulness with great courage. It is possible that some of General Longstreet's ancestors may have come from Southern France. His gasconade, as shown of late by his writings, is truly astonishing, but his courage during the war was equally remarkable. Whether his Virginia division excelled in the latter of these characteristics as much as it has for thirty-six years in the first, I will leave the readers of this monograph to decide.

If to every description of a battle, a list of casualties were added, not only would many commands, both in the army of Northern Virginia and in the army of the Potomac, which have all along been practically ignored, come well to the front; but those who for years have been reaping the glory that others sowed, would have the suspicion that perhaps after all they were rather poor creatures. Our old soldier friend, Colonel John Smith, of Jamestown, VA, to an admiring crowd, tells his story: "He carried into action five hundred men, he charged a battery, great lanes were swept through his regiment by grape and canister, whole companies were swept away, but his men close up and charge on, the carnage is appalling, but it does not appall, the guns are captured, but only he and ten men are left to hold them. His regiment has been destroyed, wiped out, annihilated," and this will go for history. But should Truth in the form of a list of casualties appear, it would be seen that Colonel Smith's command had fifteen killed and sixty wounded. That is three in the hundred killed, and twelve in the hundred wounded. Some gallantry has been displayed, some blood has been shed, but neither the one nor the other was at all phenomenal. "There were brave men before Agamemnon."

In some commands the habit of "playing possum" prevailed. When a charge was being made, if a fellow became badly frightened, all he had to do was to fall flat and play dead until his regiment passed. Afterwards he would say that the concussion from a shell had stunned him. It is needless to say that troops who were addicted to this habit stood higher abroad if their correspondent could use his pen well, than they did in the army.

Was it arrogance or was it ignorance which always caused Pickett's men to speak of the troops which marched on their left as their SUPPORTS? It is true that an order was issued and it was so published to them that they should be supported by a part of Hill's Corps, and these troops were actually formed in their rear. It is equally true that before the command to move forward was given this order was countermanded and these troops were removed and placed on their left. As these movements were seen of all men this order could not have been the origin of the belief that Pettigrew had to support them. Was it arrogance and self-conceit? It looks like it. That their division stood to Lee's army in the same relation that the sun does to the solar system. But then these people, if not blessed with some other qualities, had brains enough to know that our army could fight and conquer, too, without their assistance. They did comparatively little fighting at Second Manassas and Sharpsburg, had only two men killed at Fredericksburg, did not fire a shot at Chanellorsville, for they were miles away, and it is no exaggeration to say that they did not kill twenty of the enemy at Gettysburg.

The front line of troops, the line which does the fighting, was always known as "the line." The line which marched in rear to give moral support and practical assistance, if necessary, was in every other known body of troops called the supporting line or simply "supports." Pickett's Division had Kemper's on the right, Garnett's on the left, with Armistead's marching in the rear of Garnett's. Pettigrew's formed one line with Lane's and Scales' brigades of Pender's Division, under Trimble, marching in the rear of its right as supports. How many supporting lines did Pickett's people want? The Federals are said occasionally to have used three. Even one with us was the exception. Ordinarily one brigade of each division was held in reserve, while the others were fighting, in order to repair any possible disaster.

To show how a falsehood can be fortified by Art, I will state that I visited the Centennial Exposition at Philadelphia and there saw a very large and really fine painting representing some desperate fighting at the so-called "Bloody Angle." Clubbing with muskets, jabbing with bayonets and firing of cannon at short range, was the order of the day. Of course I knew that the subject of the painting was founded upon a myth; but had always been under the mission that while many of Pickett's and a few of Pettigrew's men were extracting the extremities of certain undergarments to be used as white flags, a part of them were keeping up a scattering fire. While before the painting a gentleman standing near me exclaimed: "Tut! "I agree to eat all the Yankees Pickett killed." Entering into conversation with him I learned that he had been at Gettysburg, had fought in Gordon's Georgia brigade, and that he did not have a very exalted opinion of Picket's men. As our Georgian friend was neither remarkably large nor hungry-looking, several persons hearing his remark stared at him. That he did exaggerate to some extent is possible, for I have since heard that among the dead men in blue, near where Armistead fell, there were six who had actually been killed by musket balls.

Colonel Fox, of Albany, N. Y., has published a work entitled, *Regimental Losses*. In it is seen a list of the twenty-seven Confederate regiments which had most men killed and wounded at Gettysburg. Readers of the histories of Pollard, Cooke and McCabe will be rather surprised to find only two Virginia regiments on this list. Those who are familiar with battlefield reports will not be surprised to see that thirteen of these regiments were from North Carolina and four from Mississippi. Three of the last named and five of the North Carolina regiments met with their loss under Pettigrew.

The North Carolina brigade had in killed and wounded eleven hundred and five, which is an average to the regiment of two hundred and seventy-six. There was not a Confederate regiment at either First or Second Manassas which equalled this average, and no Virginia regiment ever did.

This brigade on the first day met those of Biddle and Meredith, which were considered the flower of their corps, and many old soldiers say that this corps — the First — did the fiercest fighting on that day of which they ever had any experience, and the official records sustain them in this belief. Biddle's brigade was composed of one New York and three Pennsylvania regiments. Meredith's, known as the "Iron" brigade, was formed of five regiments from the west. (By the way the commander of this body, General Solomon Meredith, was a native of North Carolina, as was also General Jno. Gibbon, the famous division commander in the second corps, and North Carolina luck followed them, as they were severely wounded in this battle.) Pettigrew's brigade, with a little assistance from that of Brockenborough, after meeting these troops forced them to give ground and continued for several hours to slowly drive them 'till their ammunition became nearly exhausted. When this occurred the Federals had reached a ridge from behind which they could be supplied with the necessary ammunition. But not so with Heth's troops. The field was so open, the contending lines so close together, and as every house and barn in the vicinity was filled with sharpshooters, they could not be supplied and were in consequence relieved by two of Pender's brigades. In the meantime the enemy was reenforced by a fresh brigade of infantry and several wonderfully efficient batteries of artillery, and so when the brigades of the "right division" made their advance they suffered very severely before their opponents could be driven from the field. Meredith's brigade this day had 886 killed and wounded and 266 missing; Biddle's 642 killed and wounded and 255 missing. The loss in Brockenborough's Virginia was 148. For the whole battle, as said before, Pettigrew's killed and wounded amounted to 1,105; probably two-thirds of this loss occurred on this day.

These facts and figures are matters of record, and with these records accessible to all men, Swinton, a Northern historian, in the brilliant description he gives of the assault on the third day says that "Heth's division, commanded by Pettigrew, were all raw troops, who were only induced to make the charge by being told that they had militia to fight and that when the fire was opened upon them they raised the shout, 'The Army of the Potomac! The Army of the Potomac!' broke and fled." As after the battle the Virginia division had the guarding of several thousand Federal prisoners, captured by Carolinians and Georgians, they are probably responsible for this statement.

But to return to the fight of the first day. The Honorable Joseph Davis, then a captain in the 47th North Carolina, late Supreme Court Judge of North Carolina, speaking of this day's battle, says: "The advantage was all on the Confederate side, and I aver that this was greatly, if not chiefly, due to Pettigrew's brigade and its brave commander. The bearing of that knightly soldier and elegant scholar as he galloped along the lines in the hottest of the fight, cheering on his men, cannot be effaced from my memory."

Captain Young, of Charleston, South Carolina, a staff officer of this division, says: "No troops could have fought better than did Pettigrew's brigade on this day and I will testify on the experience of many hard fought battles, that I never saw any fight so well." Davis' brigade consisted of the 55th North Carolina, the 2nd, 11th and 42nd Mississippi. The 11th was on detached service that day. The three which fought also faced splendid troops. Here, too, was a square stand up fight in the open. During the battle these three had, besides the usual proportion of wounded, one hundred and forty-eight killed. Only two dead men were lacking to these three regiments to make their loss equal to that of ten regiments of Pickett's "magnificent Virginians."

Cutler's brigade composed of one Pennsylvania and four New York regiments was opposed to that of Davis, and its loss this day was 302 killed and wounded and 363 missing, and many of the missing were subsequently found to have been killed or severely wounded. With varying success these two brigades fought all the morning. The Federals finally gave way; but three of their regiments, after retreating for some distance, took up a new line. Two of them left the field and went to town, as the day was hot and the fire hotter. It is said they visited Gettysburg to get a little ice water. However that may be, they soon returned and fought well 'till their whole line gave way.

The ground on which these troops fought lay north of the railroad cut and was severed hundred yards from where Pettigrew's brigade was engaged with Meredith's and Biddle's. As Rode's division began to appear upon the field Davis' brigade was removed to the south side of the cut and placed in front of Stone's Pennsylvania brigade (which, having just arrived, had filled the interval between Cutler and Meredith) but did no more fighting that day. After securing; ammunition it followed the front line to the town. Had the interval between Daniel's and Scales been filled by Thomas', which was held in reserve, neither of these Carolina brigades would have suffered so severely. The 2nd and 42nd Mississippi and 55th North Carolina of Davis for the battle had 695 killed and wounded, and about two-thirds of this occurred in this first day's fight.

To illustrate the individual gallantry of these troops I will relate an adventure which came under my observation. It must be borne in mine that this brigade had been doing fierce and bloody fighting since nine o'clock and at this time not only its numerical loss but its percentage of killed and wounded was greater than that which Pickett's troops had to submit to two days later, and that it was then waiting to be relieved. Early in the afternoon of this day my division

(Rodes') arrived upon the field by the Carlisle road and at once went into action. My brigade (Daniels') was on the right, and after doing some sharp fighting, we came in sight of Heth's line, which was lying at right angles to ours as we approached. The direction of our right regiments had to be changed in order that we might move in front of their left brigade, which was Davis. The Federal line, or lines, for my impression is there were two or more of them, were also lying in the open field, the interval between the opposing lines being about three hundreds yards. Halfway between these lines was another, which ran by a house. This line was made of dead and wounded Federals, who lay "as thick as autumnal leaves which strew the brooks in Vallambrosa." It was about here that the incident occurred. A Pennsylvania regiment of Stone's brigade had then two flags — state and national — with their guard a short distance in front of them. One of these colors Sergeant Frank Price, of the 42nd Mississippi and half a dozen of his comrades determined to capture. Moving on hands and knees 'till they had nearly reached the desired object, they suddenly rose, charged and overcame the guard, captured the flag and were rapidly making off with it, when its owners fired upon them, all were struck down but the sergeant, and as he was making for the house above referred to a young staff officer in my command, having carried some message to Heth's people, was returning by a shortcut between the lines, and seeing a man with a strange flag, without noticing his uniform he thought he, too, would get a little glory along with some bunting. Dismounting among the dead and wounded he picked up and fired several muskets at Price; but was fortunate enough to miss him. Sergeant Price survived the war. His home was in Carrollton, Mississippi. Recently the information came from one of his sons, a namesake of the writer, that his gallant father was no more; he had crossed the river and was resting under the shade of the trees. The parents of Mr. Price were natives of the Old North State. Does any one who has made a study of Pickett's "magnificent division" suppose that even on the morning of the 5th when only eight hundred of the nearly or quite six thousand who had engaged in battle reported for duty, sad and depressed as they were, it could have furnished heroes like Price and his companions for such an undertaking as in spite of friends and foes was successfully accomplished? General Davis says that every field officer in his brigade was either killed or wounded. My old classmate, Major John Jones, was the only one left in the

North Carolina brigade, and he was killed in the next spring's campaign.

The following extract is taken from a description of the assault by Colonel Taylor, of General Lee's staff: "It is needless to say a word here of the heroic conduct of Pickett's division, that charge has already passed into history as one of the world's great deeds of arms." While doubtless many brave men of other commands reached the crest of the heights, this was the only organized body which entered the works of the enemy." Pickett's left and Pettigrew's and Trimble's right entered the works. Men from six brigades were there. Which command had most representatives there is a disputed point. As to the superior organization of Pickett's men what did that amount to? In the nature of things not a brigade on the field was in a condition to repel a determined attack.

Just before the final rush two bodies of Federals moved out on the field and opened fire, the one upon our right the other upon the left. The loss inflicted upon our people by these Vermonters and New Yorkers was very great, and not being able to defend themselves, there was on the part of the survivors a natural crowding to the center. The commander of a Federal brigade in his report says, "Twenty battle flags were captured in a space of one hundred yards square." This means that crowded within a space extending only one hundred yards there were the remnants of more than twenty regiments. But Colonel Taylor says that Pickett's division "was the only organized body which entered the enemy's works."

The late General Trimble said: "It will be easily understood that as Pickett's line was overlapped by the Federal lines on his right, and Pettigrew's and Trimble's front by the Federal lines on their left, each of these commands had a distinct and separate discharge of artillery and musketry to encounter, the one as incessant as the other, although Pickett's men felt its intensity sooner than the others, and were the first to be crushed under a fire before which no troops could live. While Pettigrew and Trimble suffered as much or more before the close because longer under fire, in consequence of marching farther." And again: "Both Northern and Southern descriptions of the battle of Gettysburg, in the third day's contest, have without perhaps a single exception, down to the present time, given not only most conspicuous prominence to General Pickett's division, but generally by the language used have created the impression among those not personally acquainted with the events of the day that Pickett's men did all the hard fighting, suffered the most severely and failed in their charge, because not duly and vigorously supported by the troops on their right and left. It might with as much truth be said that Pettigrew and Trimble failed in their charge, because unsupported by Pickett, who had been driven back in the crisis of their charge and was no aid to them."

Some time ago General Fitz Lee wrote a life of his uncle, General Robert E. Lee, and in a notice of this book the courteous and able editor of a leading Richmond newspaper gives a fine description of the part borne by Pickett's division in Longstreet's assault on the third day, but has little or nothing to say about the other troops engaged: whereupon a citizen of this State (North Carolina) wrote and wished to know if there were any North Carolinians upon the field when Pickett's men so greatly distinguished themselves. In answer the editor admits that he had forgotten all about the other troops engaged, and says: "We frankly confess that our mind has been from the war until now so fully possessed of the idea that the glory of the charge belonged exclusively to Pickett's division that we overlooked entirely the just measure of credit that General Fitz Lee has awarded other commands." Whereupon a correspondent of his paper, curiously enough, is in high spirits over this answer, and referring to it says: "It is especially strong in what it omits to say. The picture of the charge, as given by Swinton, as seen from the other side, would have come in perfectly; but it would have wounded our North Carolina friends and was wisely left out."

Now, as to the impertinence of this correspondent who refers to what Swinton said, there is a temptation to say something a little bitter, but as the writer has made it a rule to preserve a judicial tone as far as possible, and in presenting facts to let them speak for themselves, he refrains from gratifying a very natural inclination. Probably with no thought of malice Swinton, in making a historical flourish, sacrificed truth for the sake of a striking antithesis. This of course he knew. Equally of course this is what the correspondent did not know. No one ever accused John Swinton of being a fool.

A distinguished writer in a recent discussion of this assault says: "History is going forever to ask General Longstreet why he did not obey General Lee's orders and have Hood's and McLaws' Divisions at Pickett's back to make good the work his heroic men had done." Not so. History is not going to ask childish questions.

A Virginian writer in closing his description of this assault has recently said: "Now, this remark must occur to everyone in this connection. Pickett's breakthrough the enemy's line, led by Armistead, was the notable and prodigious thing about the whole battle of Gettysburg." If so, why so?

The commanders of Wright's Georgia and Wilcox's Alabama brigades report that when fighting on Longstreet's left on the afternoon of the second day, they carried the crest of Cemetery Ridge and captured twenty-eight cannon. The truth of this report is confirmed by General Doubleday, who says: "Wright attained the crest and Wilcox was almost in line with him. Wilcox claims to have captured twenty guns and Wright eight."

In another place he says, in speaking of a certain officer: "On his return late in the day he saw Sickle's whole line driven in and found Wright's rebel brigade established on the crest barring his way back."

Late in the same afternoon over on our left in Johnson's assault upon Culp's Hill, Stewart's brigade carried the position in their front and held it all night. Also late the same afternoon two of Early's brigades, Hoke's North Carolina and Hay's Louisiana, carried East Cemetery Heights, took many prisoners and sent them to the rear, several colors, and captured or silenced twenty guns (spiking some of them before they fell back). And a part of them maintained their position for over an hour, some of them having advanced as far as the Baltimore Pike. It is an undoubted fact that even after their brigades had fallen back parts of the 9th Louisiana and 6th North Carolina, under Major Tate, held their position at the wall on the side of the hill (repelling several attacks) for an hour, thus holding open the gate to Cemetery Heights, and it does seem that under cover of night this gate might have been used and the Ridge occupied by a strong force of our troops with slight loss.

On the afternoon of the third day the men who were in front of the narrow space abandoned by the enemy, and some who were on their right and left, in a disorganized mass of about one thousand, crowded into this space for safety. (Less than fifty followed Armistead to the abandoned gun.) When, after about ten minutes, they were attacked they either surrendered or fled. No one knows what State had most representatives in this "crowd" as the Federal Col. Hall calls them, but the man who wrote that they did "the notable and prodigious thing about the whole battle of Gettysburg" thinks he knows. All soldiers now know, and many knew then, that in sending 9,000 or 10,000 men to attack the army of the Potomac, concentrated and strongly fortified, there was no reasonable hope of success.

The thing of most interest to readers of history is the question to which of the troops engaged on that ill-starred field is to be awarded the palm for heroic endurance and courageous endeavor. To know the percentage of killed and wounded of the different troops engaged in this assault, is to know which are entitled to most honor. Some of the troops in Pettigrew's division met with a loss of more than 60 percent. The percentage for Pickett's division was not quite 28. The 11th Mississippi, as said elsewhere, was the only regiment in Pettigrew's or Trimble's divisions, which entered the assault fresh. Most of the other troops of these commands had been badly cut up in the first day's battle, and the exact number they carried into the assault is not known, but entering fresh the number taken in by the Eleventh is known, and the number it lost in killed and wounded is reported by Dr. Guild. Consequently there cannot be the slightest doubt that its percentage of loss for the assault was at least 60. It is fair to presume that the percentage in the other regiments of its brigade was equally great. It is also fair to presume that the brigade immediately on its right, which went somewhat farther and stayed somewhat longer under the same terrific fire, lost as heavily.

If the charge of the Light Brigade at Balaklava in which it lost 35 percent, has rendered it famous, why should not the charge of Davis' brigade in which it lost 60 percent, render it equally famous? And if the blundering stupidity of the order to charge has excited our sympathy in behalf of the British cavalry, is there not enough of that element in the order to the infantry brigade to satisfy the most exacting? And if Davis' brigade deserves fame why do not all the brigades — with one exception — of Pettigrew and Trimble also deserve it?

Colonel W. E. Potter, of the 12th New Jersey, Smyth's brigade, Hay's division, in an address delivered several years ago, after speaking in very complimentary terms of the conduct of the North Carolina and Mississippi brigades of Pettigrew's division, says: "Again a larger number of the enemy was killed and wounded in front of

Smyth than in front of Webb. Of this, besides the general recollection of all of us who were then present, I have special evidence. I rode over the field covered by the fire of these two brigades on the morning of Sunday, July 5th, in company with Lt. Colonel Chas. H. Morgan, the chief of staff of Gen. Hancock, and Capt. Hazard. As we were passing the front of Smyth's brigade, Col. Morgan said to Hazard: 'They may talk as they please about the hard fighting in front of Gibbon, but there are more dead men here than anywhere in our front.' To this conclusion Hazard assented."

After the frightful ordeal they had been through it is not to the discredit of any of the troops engaged to say that when they reached the breastworks, or their vicinity, there was no fight left in them, for there is a limit to human endurance. This limit had been reached, and this is shown by the fact that there was not an organization upon the field which, when an attack was made on its flank, made the slightest attempt to change front to meet it, but either surrendered or fled. This being the case the only thing of interest is to decide which brigades received the most punishment before this limit was reached.

During the recent discussion in the Richmond newspapers as to whether any of the North Carolina troops reached a point at or near the enemy's works, the most prominent writer on the negative side of the question gives extracts from the reports of certain participants in the charge to corroborate his opinion, and by a singular oversight gives one from the report of Major John Jones, then commanding Pettigrew's own brigade, who says: "The brigade dashed on, and many had reached the wall when we received a deadly volley from the left." To have reached the stonewall on the left of the salient, they must necessarily have advanced considerably farther than any troops on the field. And yet the above writer in the face of Major Jones' testimony, thinks that neither his nor any North Carolina troops were there. But then he quotes from the Federal Col. Hall, "who," he says, "gives a list of the flags captured by his command when the charge was made." Amongst them he mentions that of the 22nd North Carolina, and says: "If this can be accepted as true it of course ends all controversy." Col. Hall reports that at the close of the assault his brigade captured the flags of the 14th, 18th, 19th and 57th Virginia, and that of the 22nd North Carolina. Webb reports that his command captured six flags, but does not name the regiments to which they belonged. Heth captured those of the 1st, 7th and 28th Virginia. Carroll's brigade those of the 34th North Carolina and 38th Virginia. Smyth's brigade those of 1st and 14th Tennessee, 16th and 52nd North Carolina and five others, the names not given, and Sherrill's brigade captured three, the names not given. Thus we have the names of eight Virginia, four North Carolina and two Tennessee and fourteen reported captured, names not given. In all twenty-eight, which accounts for Pickett's fifteen, Scales' five, Pettigrew's own three and Archer's four. One of Pettigrew's and one of Archer's having been carried back, some of the other troops must have lost one. If official reports which say that the flags of the 1st and 14th Tennessee, and of the 16th, 22nd, 34th and 52nd North Carolina were captured, cannot be accepted as true and thus "end all controversy," perhaps a restatement of the fact that twenty-eight colors were taken at the close of the assault may do so, for as said above the Virginia division had only fifteen flags.

To show the disproportion that existed at the close of the fight between the numbers of men and flags, one officer reports that his regiment charged upon the retreating rebels and captured five regimental battle flags and over forty prisoners, and a brigade commander speaking of the ground at and in front of the abandoned works, says: "Twenty battle flags were captured in a space of 100 yards square."

There is one fact that should be remembered in connection with this assault, namely: That of all breastworks, a stonewall inspires most confidence and its defenders will generally fire deliberately and accurately and cling to it tenaciously.

The stonewall ran from the left and in front of Lane's, Davis' and Pettigrew's North Carolina brigades and ended where the right of the last named rested at the close of the assault. At this point works made of rails covered with earth began and ran straight to the front for some distance and then made a sharp turn to the left in the direction of Round Top, continuing in nearly a straight line beyond Pickett's right. It was a short distance to the right of the outer corner of these works when Webb's men gave way.

Several years ago there was published in the *Philadelphia Times*, an article by Colonel W. W. Wood, of Armistead's brigade, giving his recollections of this affair. As the writer had very naively made several confessions, which I had never seen made by any other of Pickett's men, and had evidently intended to speak truthfully, I put the paper aside for future reference. I shall now make several selections from it and endeavor to criticise them fairly. Our artillery crowned the ridge, and behind it sheltered by the hills lay our infantry: "The order to go forward was obeyed with alacrity and cheerfulness, for we believed that the battle was practically over, and that we had nothing to do but to march unopposed to Cemetery Heights and occupy them. While making the ascent it was seen that the supports to our right and left flanks were not coming forward as we had been told they would. Mounted officers were seen dashing frantically up and down their lines, apparently endeavoring to get them to move forward, but we could see that they would not move. Their failure to support us was discouraging, but it did not dishearten us. Some of our men cursed them for cowards, etc." So far no great courage had been required.

But what troops were they that Pickett's people were cursing for cowards? On the right they were Perry's Florida and Wilcox's Alabama, under the command of the latter general. Their orders were that when twenty minutes had elapsed after the line had started they were to march straight ahead and repel any body of flankers who should attack the right. This order was obeyed to the letter. At the required time they moved forward and kept moving. About where Pickett should have been (Pickett's line had previously obliqued to the left) not a Confederate was to be seen. They kept on and single handed and alone attacked the whole Federal army, then exulting in victory. Of course they were repulsed, but when they knew they were beaten did they surrender that they might be sheltered in Northern prisons from Northern bullets? Not they. They simply fell back and made their way, as best they could, to the Confederate lines. Is there any significance in the facts that shortly after this battle General Wilcox was promoted and General Pickett and his men were sent out of the army? What other troops were they whom these men were cursing for being cowards? Some of them were the choice troops of A. P. Hill's old division, ever famous for its fighting qualities, others were the survivors of Archer's brigade of gallant Tennesseans, Mississippians, brave and impetuous, North Carolinians, always steady, always true. These men were cursed as cowards, and by Pickett's Virginians! Achilles cursed by Thersites! A lion barked at by a cur.

But there was one brigade, and only one, in Pettigrew's division which failed in the hour of trial. It was from their own state, and had once been an efficient body of soldiers, and even on this occasion something might be said in its defense. But had this not been the case, to the men of Armistead's brigade (who were doing the cursing) the memory of their own behavior at Sharpsburg and Shepherdstown should have had the effect of making them charitable towards the shortcomings of others.

Let us allow the colonel to continue: "From the time the charge began unto this moment, not a shot had been fired at us nor had we been able to see, because of the density of the smoke, which hung over the battlefield like a pall, that there was an enemy in front of us. The smoke now lifted from our front and there, right before us, scarcely two hundred yards away, stood Cemetery Heights in awful grandeur. At their base was a double line of Federal infantry and several pieces of artillery, posted behind stonewalls, and to the right and left of them both artillery and infantry supports were hurriedly coming up. The situation was indeed appalling, though it did not seem to appall. The idea of retreat did not seem to occur to any one. Having obtained a view of the enemy's position, the men now advanced at the double quick, and for the first time since the charge began they gave utterance to the famous Confederate yell." So it seems that all that has been spoken and written about their having marched one thousand yards under the fire of one hundred cannon and twenty thousand muskets, is the veriest bosh and nonsense. They marched eight hundred yards as safely as if on parade. When the smoke lifted they charged for two hundred yards towards the breastworks; the left only reached it — the right never did, but lay down in the field and there and then fifteen hundred of them "threw down their muskets for the war." Colonel Wood continues: "The batteries to the right and left of Cemetery Heights now began to rain grapeshot and canister upon us, and the enemy's infantry at the base of the Heights, poured volley after volley into our ranks. The carnage was indeed terrible; but still the division, staggering and bleeding, pushed on towards the Heights they had been ordered to take. Of course such terrible slaughter could not last long. The brave little division did not number men enough to make material for prolonged slaughter."

The carnage was for them indeed terrible, and their subsequent behavior up to their defeat and rout at Five Forks, showed that they never forgot it. Let us see what was this horrible carnage. The fifteen regiments, according to General Longstreet, carried into the charge, of officers and men, forty-nine hundred. It is more probable that the number was fifty-five hundred. If they had the former number their percentage of killed and wounded was nearly twenty-eight, if the latter, not quite twenty-five. On the first day the North Carolina brigade lost thirty and on the third, sixty percent. The "brave, the magnificent" when they had experienced a loss of fifteen killed to the regiment, became sick of fighting, as the number surrendered shows. One regiment of the "cowards," the 42nd Mississippi, only after it had met with a loss of sixty killed and a proportionate number of wounded, concluded that it was about time to rejoin their friends. Another regiment of the "cowards," the 26th North Carolina, only after it had more men killed and wounded than any one of the two thousand seven hundred Federal and Confederate regiments ever had, came to the same conclusion. The five North Carolina regiments of this division had five more men killed than Pickett's fifteen.

To continue: "In a few brief moments more the left of Armistead's brigade, led by himself on foot, had passed beyond the stonewall, and were among the guns of the enemy, posted in rear of it. General Garnet had before then been instantly killed, and General Kemper had been severely wounded, the survivors of their brigades had become amalgamated with Armistead's." How can any one see any organization to boast of here? "Our line of battle was not parallel to the Heights, and the left of the diminished line reached the Heights first. The right of the line never reached them. The men of the right, however, were near enough to see General Armistead shot down near a captured gun as he was waving his sword above his head, and they could see men surrendering themselves as prisoners. Just then a detachment of Federal infantry came out flanking our right, and shouted to us to surrender. There was nothing else to do, except to take the chance, which was an extremely good one, of being killed on the retreat back over the hill. But a few, myself among the number, rightly concluded that the enemy was weary of carnage, determined to run the risk of getting back to the Confederate lines. Our retreat was made singly, and I at least was not fired upon." If the division had equalled Colonel Wood in gallantry, it would not have surrendered more sound men than it had lost in killed and wounded, as by taking some risk the most of those captured might have escaped as he did. The colonel concludes: "When the retreat commenced on the night of the 4th of July, the nearly three hundred men who had been confined in the various brigade guard houses were released from confinement, and they and their guard permitted to return to duty in the ranks, and many detailed men were treated in the same way. On the morning of the 5th of July, the report of the division showed not quite eleven hundred present. Eleven hundred from forty-five hundred leaves thirty-four hundred, and that was the number of casualties suffered by Pickett's little division at Gettysburg." I have known individuals who took pride in poverty and disease. The surrender of soldiers in battle was often unavoidable; but I have never known a body of troops other than Pickett's, who prided themselves upon that misfortune. General Pemberton or Marshal Bazaine may have done so. If they did, their countrymen did not agree with them, and it is well for the fame of General Lee and his army that the belief that the road to honor lay in that direction, was not very prevalent. Pickett's division has been compared to a "lance-head of steel," which pierced the centre of the Federal army. To be in accord with the comparison, it was always represented as being smaller than it really was.

Colonel Wood, at the conclusion of his article, puts its strength at 4,500 officers and men, at the beginning at 4,500 "men." This last would agree with General Longstreet's estimate of 4,900 effectives. Knowing as I do the average per brigade of Jackson's Veterans — one-half of the army — and that they had been accustomed to fight two days for every one day fought by Longstreet's men, I think it probable that Pickett's brigade must have averaged nearly, if not quite, two thousand.

But I will place the strength of the division at fifty-five hundred. I have heard that fifteen hundred were surrendered. Official records say that thirteen hundred and sixty-four were killed and wounded.

According to Colonel Wood, leaving out the three hundred guardhouse men, eight hundred appeared for duty on the morning of the 5th. These three numbers together make thirty-six hundred and sixty-four, which taken from fifty-five hundred leaves eighteen hundred and thirty-six, and this was the number of men which the "brave little division" had to run away. They ran and ran and kept running 'till the high waters in the Potomac stopped them. As they ran they shouted "that they were all dead men, that Pettigrew had failed to support them, and that their noble division had been swept away." The outcry they made was soon heard all over Virginia, and its echo is still heard in the North.

After our army had recrossed the river and had assembled at Bunker Hill, the report that Pickett's division of "dead men" had drawn more rations than any division in the army, excited a good deal of good-natured laughter. Among the officers of our army, to whom the casualty lists were familiar, the question was often discussed, why it was that some of Pettigrew's brigades, marching over the same ground at the same time, should have suffered so much more than General Pickett's? This question was never satisfactorily answered 'till after the war. The mystery was then explained by the Federal General Doubleday, who made the statement that "all the artillery supporting Webb's brigade (which being on the right of Gibbons' division, held the projecting wall) excepting one piece, was destroyed, and nearly all of the artillerymen either killed or wounded by the cannonade which preceded the assault."

Of course there were exceptions, but the general rule was that those troops who suffered the most themselves inflicted the greatest loss on the enemy and were consequently the most efficient. Colonel Fox says: "The history of a battle or war should be studied in connection with the figures which show the losses. By overlooking them, an indefinite and often erroneous idea is obtained. By overlooking them many historians fail to develop the important points of the contest: they use the same rhetorical descriptions for different attacks, whether the pressure was strong or weak, the loss great or small, the fight bloody or harmless." As it was the custom in some commands to report every scratch as a wound, and in others to report no man as wounded who was fit for duty, the most accurate test for courage and efficiency is the number of killed. In the eight brigades and three regiments from Virginia in this battle, three hundred and seventy-five were killed, and nineteen hundred and seventy-one wounded. That is for every one killed five and twenty-five hundredths were reported wounded. In the seven brigades and three regiments from North Carolina, six hundred and ninety-six were killed and three thousand and fifty-four wounded. That is for every man killed only four and forty hundredths appeared on the list as wounded.

If it be a fact that from Gettysburg to the close of the war, among the dead upon the various battlefields comparatively few representatives from the Virginian infantry were to be found, it is not always necessarily to their discredit. For instance, even at Gettysburg two such brigades as Mahone's and Smyth's had respectively only seven and fourteen men killed. It was not for them to say whether they were to advance or be held back. Their duty was to obey orders. In the same battle two of Rodes' North Carolina brigades — Daniels' and Iverson's — had between them two hundred and forty-six men buried upon the field. Here we see that the eight regiments and one battalion, which formed these two North Carolina commands, had twenty-two more men killed than Pickett's fifteen. And yet Virginia history does not know that they were even present at this battle.

Now, for a brief recapitulation. The left of Garnett's and Armistead's brigades, all of Archer's and Scales' (but that all means very few, neither of them at the start being larger than a full regiment) a few of the 37th and the right of Pettigrew's own brigade took possession of the works, which the enemy had abandoned on their approach. Pettigrew's and Trimble's left and Pickett's right lay out in the field on each flank of the projecting work and in front of the receding wall, and from forty to fifty yards from it. There they remained for a few minutes, 'till a fresh line of the enemy, which had been lying beyond the crest of the ridge, approached. Then being attacked on both flanks, and knowing how disorganized they were, our men made no fight, but either retreated or surrendered. Archer's, Scales' and Pettigrew's own brigade went as far and stayed as long or longer than any of Pickett's. Davis' brigade, while charging impetuously ahead of the line was driven back, when it had reached a point about one hundred yards from the enemy. Lane's, the left brigade, remained a few moments longer than any of the other troops and retired in better order.

Now, it must not be inferred from anything in this paper that there has been any intention to reflect upon all Virginia infantry. Far from it. The three regiments in Stenart's mixed brigade and Mahone's brigade were good troops. Perhaps there were others equally good. But there was one brigade which was their superior, as it was the superior of most of the troops in General Lee's array. And that was Smith's brigade of Early's division. These troops in spite of the Richmond newspapers and the partiality of certain of their commanders, had no superiors in any army. Never unduly elated by prosperity, never depressed by adversity, they were even to the last, when enthusiasm had entirely fled and hope was almost dead, the models of what good soldiers should be.

"It is not precisely those who know how to kill," says Dragomiroff, "but those who death's know how to die, who are all-powerful the test, on a field of battle."

Regiments that had twenty-nine or more officers and men killed on the field in certain battles:

Regiment	Brigade	Battle	Killed
13 Ga.	Lawton	Sharpsburg	48
3 N. C.	Ripley	"	46
1 Texas.	Wofford	"	45
13 N. C.	Garland	"	41
30 Va.	Walker	"	39
48 N. C.	Walker	"	31
27 N. C.	Walker	"	31
50 Ga.	Drayton	"	29
57 N. C.	Law	Fredericksburg.	32
2 N. C.	Ramseur	Chancellorsville.	47
4 N. C.	Ramseur	"	45
3 N. C.	Colston	"	38
7 N. C.	Lane.	"	37
1 N. C.	Colston	"	34
37 N. C.	Lane	"	34.
23 N. C.	Iverson	"	32
13 N. C.	Pender	"	31
22 N. C.	Pender	"	30.
51 Ga.	Semmes	"	30
4 Ga.	Doles	"	29
18 N. C.	Lane	"	30
26 N. C.	Pettigrew	Gettysburg.	86
42 Miss.	Davis	"	60
11 N. C.	Pettigrew	"	50

2 Miss.	Davis	"	49
45 N. C.	Daniel	"	46
23 N. C.	Iverson	"	41
17 Miss.	Barksdale	"	40
55 N. C.	Davis	"	39
59 Va.	Armistead	"	35
52 N. C.	Pettigrew	"	33
11 Ga.	Anderson	"	32
5 N. C.	Iverson	"	31
13 S. C.	Perrin	"	31
13 N. C.	Scales	"	29
2 N. C. Batt.	Daniel	"	29
3 N. C. Batt.	Steuart	"	29
20 N. C. Batt.	Iverson	"	29

The proportion of wounded to killed was 4.8 to one. That is, if 100 are killed 480 will be wounded. When 100 men are killed, there will be among the wounded 64 who will die of wounds. While this may not always be the case in a single regiment, yet when a number of regiments are taken together the wonderful law of averages makes these proportions rules about which there is no varying.

There is an old saw which says that "it takes a soldier's weight in lead and iron to kill him." Most people believe that this saying has to be taken with many grains of allowance, but it was shown during the war to be literally true. In the battle of Murfreesboro the weight of the 20,307 projectiles fired by the Federal artillery was 225,000 pounds, and that of the something over 2,000,000 musket balls exceeded 150,000 pounds and their combined weight exceeded that of the 2,319 Confederates who were killed or mortally wounded.

In the Federal armies deaths from wounds amounted to 110,000 and from disease and all other causes about 250,000, a total of about 360,000. For deaths in the Southern armies only an approximation can be arrived at. Probably 100,000 died of wounds and as many more of disease, a total of about 200,000 which added to the Federal loss, makes about 560,000. This number of soldiers drawn up in battle array would make a line 112 miles long.

Webb's Philadelphia Brigade and other troops

With singular inappropriateness this brigade and several other Federal organizations have erected monuments to commemorate their gallantry upon the third day's battlefield. It would appear that they should have been erected on the spot where their gallantry was displayed. It does not require much courage to lie behind breastworks and shoot down an enemy in an open field and then to run away, as it and the other troops in its vicinity did, when that enemy continued to approach. But, while it does not add to their fame, it is not to their discredit that they did give way. For however much discipline and inherent qualities may extend it, there is a limit to human endurance, and they had suffered severely, Webb's brigade in three days having lost forty-nine percent. If there ever have been troops serving in a long war who never on any occasion gave way till they had lost as heavily, they were the superiors of any in Napoleon's or Wellington's armies. The loss in the British infantry at Salamanca was only twelve percent. That of the "Light Brigade" at Balaklava was only thirty-seven. That of Pickett's only twenty-eight, and they were ruined forever. It is true the North Carolina and Mississippi brigades of Heth's division lost in the first day's battle about thirty and on the third at least sixty percent, and this without having their morale seriously impaired, but then both of these organizations were composed of exceptionally fine troops.

Heth's Division

This division was composed of Archer's Tennessee and Alabama regiments, Pettigrew's North Carolina, Davis' Mississippi and Brockenborough's Virginia brigades.

Counting from right to left, Archer joining Pickett's left, this was the order in which they were formed for the third day's assault. Soon after the order to advance was given the left brigade gave way. The others advanced and did all that flesh and blood could do. General Hooker, who has written the Confederate military history for the Mississippi troops, quotes from Dr. Ward, a surgeon who witnessed the assault, who says that the fire of Cemetery Hill, having been concentrated upon Heth's division, he saw no reason why North Carolina, Mississippi, Tennessee and Alabama troops should not participate in whatever honors that were won on that day; for, says he, all soldiers know that the number killed is the one and only test for pluck and endurance. General Hooker then states, "The brigades in the army which lost most heavily in killed and wounded at Gettysburg, was (1) Pettigrew's North Carolina, (2) Davis' Mississippi and North Carolina, (3) Daniels' North Carolina and (4) Barksdale's Mississippi." These four had an average of 837 killed and wounded. Pickett's three brigades had an average of 455.

Percentages

Some have contended the number of deaths and wounds is the test for endurance, others the percentage is the true test. It may be neither the one nor the other alone, but that rather both together should be taken into account. The same percentage in a large regiment should count for more than that in a small one. For while only one Confederate brigade is reported to have reached as high as 63 percent, the regiment, the smaller organizations, more frequently attained that rate. Thirteen are known and several others are supposed to have reached it. And as to the company, there was hardly a hard fought battle in which at least one did not have nearly every man killed or wounded. The writer knows of four in as many North Carolina regiments which in one battle were almost destroyed. In three of these the percentage went from eighty-seven to ninety-eight, and the fourth had every officer and man struck. Taking Colonel Fox's tables for authority, we find that of the thirty-four regiments standing highest on the percentage list six were from North Carolina, and these six carried into battle two thousand nine hundred and nine; only two of the thirty-four were from Virginia, and their "present" was fifty-five for one and one hundred and twenty-eight for the other. Tennessee, leading the list in number, has seven, Georgia and Alabama each has six. The two states, whose soldiers Virginia historians with a show of generosity were in the habit of so frequently complimenting, Texas and Louisiana, make rather a poor show — the former has only one regiment on the list and the other does not appear at all.

The 26th North Carolina had 820 officers and men at Gettysburg, and their percentage of killed and wounded was exceeded by that of only two Confederate and three Federal regiments during the whole war, and those five were all small, ranging from one hundred and sixty-eight to two hundred and sixty-eight. As Senator Vance's old regiment unquestionably stands head on the numerical list, so should it, in the opinion of the writer, stand on that of percentages.

As, for reasons not necessary to mention here, this list relates almost entirely to the early battles of the war, it is not as satisfactory as it might be. Though North Carolina should head the list in the greatest percentage in any one regiment, it does not in the number of regiments. Early in the war, when it was generally believed that peace would come before glory enough to go round had been obtained, the North Carolina troops were, to a certain extent, held back. For this reason, however flattering to our State pride, Colonel Fox's table is, as it stands, it would have been vastly more so had it covered the whole war, especially the last year, when the fortunes of the Confederacy, were held up by the bright bayonets of the soldiers from the Old North State.

"Carolina, Carolina, Heaven's blessings attend her!"

"A Poor Thing, But Mine Own"

We see in field returns for February and March, 1865, that Pickett's division was the largest in the army. There is nothing remarkable about this fact, for they were not engaged in the bloody repulse at Bristoe Station, were not, present at the Wilderness, were not present at Spottsylvania, and did not serve in those horrible trenches at Petersburg. In the same report we see that their aggregate, present and absent, was 9,487. It may be that since the world was made there has been a body of troops with 9,000 names on their muster rolls, who, serving in a long and bloody war, inflicted so little loss upon their enemy or suffered so little themselves. It may be, but it is not probable. With one exception no division surrendered so few men at Appomattox.

Col. Dodge, of Boston, in his history speaks of the commander of this division as "the Ney of Lee's army." If satire is intended it is uncalled for as the Virginian never inflicted any loss upon the enemy worth mentioning; certainly not enough to cause any Yankee to owe him a grudge.

Davis' Brigade

This brigade was composed of the 2nd, 11th and 42nd Mississippi and 55th North Carolina. The two first were veteran. They had fought often and always well. The 42nd Mississippi and 55th North Carolina were full regiments, Gettysburg being their first battle of importance. The two first named served in Law's brigade of Hood's division at

Sharpsburg or Antietam, where they greatly distinguished themselves, as they had before at First Manassas and Gain's Mill. The 11th Mississippi was the only fresh regiment outside of Pickett's division which took part in the assault of July 3rd, so all of its loss occurred on that day, that loss being 202 killed and wounded. The number they carried in is variously stated at from 300 to 350. If the one, the percentage of their loss was 67, if the other, 57.

Pender's Division

This famous division, consisting of two North Carolina, one Georgia and one South Carolina brigade, was first commanded by Lieutenant General A. P. Hill (who was killed just at the close of the war), after his promotion by Pender, who was killed at Gettysburg, and afterwards by Wilcox.

Rodes' Division

At this time this division consisted of three North Carolina, one Georgia and one Alabama brigade. It was first commanded by Lieutenant General D. H. Hill, who was promoted and transferred to the West. Then by Rodes, who was killed at Winchester, then by Grimes, who was assassinated just after the war. Just after Gettysburg, General Lee told General Rodes that his division had accomplished more in this battle than any other in his army. The record this body made in the campaign of 1864 has never been equalled. It had more men killed and wounded than it ever carried into any one action. The records show this.

Johnson's Division

This division was composed for the most part of Virginians. It had only two North Carolina regiments, the 1st and 3rd. During the Mine Run campaign General Ewell and General Johnson were together when a Federal battery opened fire upon the division and became very annoying. What did these Virginia generals do about it? "Only this and nothing more." The corps commander quietly remarked to the division commander: "Why don't you send your North Carolina regiments after that battery and bring it in?" At once these regiments were selected from the line, and were forming to make a charge, when the battery was withdrawn.

What the Troops from the Different States Considered Bloody Work

The seven Confederate regiments, which had most men killed in any battle of the war, were the 6th Alabama, ninety-one, killed; 26th North Carolina, eighty-six; 1st South Carolina Rifles, eighty-one; 4th North Carolina, seventy-seven; 44th Georgia, seventy-one; 14th Alabama, seventy-one; and 20th North Carolina, seventy. Pickett's "veterans" must have thought that to have nine or ten men to the regiment killed, was an evidence of severe fighting, for the most of them think even to this day, that to have had nearly fifteen to the regiment killed at Gettysburg was a carnage so appalling as to amount to butchery.

Iverson's Brigade

This brigade consisted of the 5th, 12th, 20th and 23rd North Carolina. It was first commanded by Garland, who was killed in the Maryland campaign, then by Iverson, then by Bob Johnson, then by Toon. The 20th was a fine regiment. At a very critical time at Gain's Mill, it captured a battery. It is on Colonel Fox's list as having had on that occasion seventy killed and two-hundred and two wounded. Equally good was the 12th. That brilliant and lamented young officer, General R. E. Rodes, once made a little speech to this regiment in which he said that after Gettysburg General Lee had told him that his division had accomplished more in that battle than any division in his army, and that he himself would say that the 12th North Carolina was the best regiment in his division. Only last week, while visiting a neighboring town, I saw a bald headed old fellow, who was Color Sergeant of this regiment at Chancellorsville. It was charging a battery when its commander, Major Rowe, was killed and for a moment it faltered. Just then it was that Sergeant Whitehead rushed to the front with the exclamation: "Come on 12th, I'm going to ram this flag down one of them guns." The regiment answered with a yell, took the battery and held it.

In the Seven Days' battle this regiment had 51 men killed on the field. It suffered most at Malvern Hill, where private Tom Emry of this county was complimented in orders and promoted for gallantry.

General Hancock having witnessed a very gallant, but unsuccessful charge of the 5th N. C. at Williamsburg, complimented it in the highest terms. Lieutenant Tom Snow of this county — a Chapel Hill boy — was killed on this occasion and his body was delivered to his friends by the Federals.

With such Colonels as Chirstie, Blacknall and Davis — the first two dying of wounds — the 23rd could not fail in always being an "A No. 1" Regiment. This brigade at Gettysburg had one hundred and eleven killed, and three hundred and forty-four wounded.

In the fall of 1864 near Winchester, General Bradley Johnston of Maryland was a witness of the conduct of this brigade under very trying circumstances, and he has recently written a very entertaining account of what he saw, and in it he is very enthusiastic in his praise of their courage and discipline, comparing them to Sir Colin Campbell's "Thin Red Line" at Balaklava.

Daniels' Brigade

This brigade consisted of the 32nd, 43rd, 45th, 53rd and 2nd battalion, all from North Carolina. It was first commanded by Daniels, who was killed at Spottsylvania. Then by Grimes and after his promotion by Colonels, several of whom were killed. To say that this brigade accomplished more in the first day's battle than any other, is no reflection upon the other gallant brigades of Rode's division. General Doubleday, who, after the fall of General Reynolds, succeeded to the command of the First Corps, says that Stone's Pennsylvania brigade held the key-point of this day's battle. These Pennsylvanians, occupying a commanding position, were supported by other regiments of infantry and two batteries of artillery. Daniels' right, Brabble's 32nd North Carolina leading, had the opportunity given it to carry this "key-point" by assault, and gloriously did it take advantage of that opportunity. No troops ever fought better than did this entire brigade, and its killed and wounded was greater by far than any brigade in its corps. The 45th and 2nd battalion met with the greatest loss, the former having 219 killed and wounded, the latter 153 out of 240, which was nearly 64 percent. When, on the morning of the 12th of May at Spottsylvania, Hancock's corps ran over Johnson's Division, capturing or scattering the whole command, this fine brigade and Ramseur's North Carolina, and Bob Johnston's North Carolina, by their promptness and intrepidity, checked the entire Second Corps and alone held it 'till Lane's North Carolina, Harris' Mississippi and other troops could be brought up.

Ramseur's Brigade

This famous brigade consisted of the 2nd, 4th, 14th and 30th North Carolina. It was first commanded by General George B. Anderson, who was killed at Sharpsburg. Then by Ramseur, who was promoted and killed at Cedar Creek. Then by Cox. The fondness of this brigade for prayer meeting and Psalm singing united with an ever readiness to fight, reminds one of Cromwell's Ironsides. It fought well at Seven Pines when one of its regiments, having carried in six hundred and seventy-eight officers and men, lost fifty-four percent, in killed and wounded. At Malvern Hill it met with great loss. It occupied the bloody lane at Sharpsburg. At Chancellorsville out of fifteen hundred and nine, it had one hundred and fifty-four killed and five hundred and twenty-six wounded, or forty-five per cent, On the 12th of May at Spottsylvania it acted probably the most distinguished part of any brigade in the army. It did the last fighting at Appomattox, and about twenty-five men of the 14th, under Captain W. T. Jenkins, of Halifax County, fired the last shots. To see these poor devils, many of them almost barefooted and all of them half starved, approach a field where a battle was raging was a pleasant sight. The crack of Napoleons, the roar of Howitzers and crash of musketry always excited and exhilarated them, and as they swung into action they seemed supremely happy.

Lane's Brigade

Lane's brigade consisted of the 7th, 18th, 28th, 33rd and 37th North Carolina. It was first commanded by General L. O. B. Branch, who was killed at Sharpsburg. The 7th and 18th appear upon Colonel Fox's percentage table, both having in the Seven Days' fight lost 56 percent. The numerical loss for the brigade was 807. At Chancellorsville it had 739 killed and wounded. In the history of this battle by Col. Hamlin, of Maine, the conduct of this brigade is spoken of very highly. In Longstreet's assault as it moved over the field the two wings of its right regiment parted company, and at the close of the assault were several hundred yards apart. The point of direction for the assaulting column was a small cluster of trees opposite to and in front of Archer's brigade, and while the rest of the line dressed on this brigade, by some misunderstanding, four and a half regiments of Lane's dressed to the left. It went some distance beyond the Emmittsburg Road, but fell back to that road, where it remained fighting 'till all the rest of the line had given way, when it was withdrawn by General Trimble.

Some time ago a Union veteran in a St. Louis paper gave an account of what came under his observation at Spottsylvania. His command had been repulsed and was being driven by Lane's brigade, when he was shot down. As the victorious line swept by a Confederate was struck, falling near him. The conduct of a young officer, whose face was radiant with the joy of battle, had attracted his attention, and he asked his wounded neighbor who he was. His reply was, "That's Capt. Billy McLaurin, of the 18th North Carolina, the bravest man in Lee's army."

Archer's Brigade

This superb brigade consisted of three regiments from Tennessee, one regiment and one battalion from Alabama. It suffered very severely the first day; on the third it was gallantly led by Colonel Frye, who says, referring to the close of the assault: "I heard Garnett give a command. Seeing my gesture of inquiry he called out, 'I am dressing on you.' A few seconds later he fell dead. A moment later a shot through my thigh prostrated me. The smoke soon became so dense that I could see but little of what was going on before me. A moment later I heard General Pettigrew calling to rally them on the left (referring to a brigade which had just given way). All of the five regimental colors of my command reached the line of the enemy's works, and many of my officers and men were killed after passing over it." Colonel Shepherd, who succeeded Colonel Frye in command, said in his official report that every flag in Archer's brigade, except one, was captured at or within the works of the enemy. This brigade and Pettigrew's were awarded the honor of serving as a rear guard when the army recrossed the river.

Hoke's Brigade

Two of General Early's brigades made a very brilliant charge on the second day: but being unsupported were forced to fall back. They were Hoke's North Carolina, commanded by Colonel Avery, who was killed, and Hayes' Louisiana. They did equally well in every respect, yet one is always praised, the other rarely mentioned. Hoke's brigade consisted of the 6th, 21st, 54th and 57th. First commanded by Hoke, after his promotion by Godwin, who was killed in the Valley, and then by Gaston Lewis.

The 54th was on detached duty and did not take part in this battle. Mr. Vandersliee, in his fine description of this affair, does full justice to our North Carolina boys, and closes by saying: "It will be noted that while this assault is called that of the 'Louisiana Tigers,' the three North Carolina regiments lost more men than the five Louisiana regiments."

Pay Your Money And Take Your Choice

From a book recently published, entitled, *Pickett and His Men*, the following paragraph is taken: "Pettigrew was trying to reach the post of death and honor, but he was far away and valor could not annihilate space. His troops had suffered cruelly in the battle the day before and their commander had been wounded. They were now led by an officer ardent and brave, but to them unknown."

Col. Carswell McClellan, who was an officer of Gen. Humphreys' staff, comparing the assault made by this general at Fredericksburg with that which is known as Pickett's, says: "As the bugle sounded the 'charge,' Gen. Humphreys turned to his staff, and bowing with uncovered head, remarked as quietly and as pleasantly as if inviting them to be seated around his table, 'Gentlemen, I shall lead this charge. I presume, of course, you will wish to ride with me.'" Now, compare that to Pickett, who was not within a mile of his column when they charged at Gettysburg — Pettigrew and Armistead led Pickett's division there. Of this grand assault of Humphreys I can do no better than quote Gen. Hooker's report: "This attack was made with a spirit and determination seldom, if ever, equalled in war. Seven of Gen. Humphreys' staff officers started with the charge, five were dismounted before reaching the line where Gen. Couch's troops were lying, and four were wounded before the assault ceased."

The School Girl's Hero

But as he spoke Pickett, at the head of his division, rode over the crest of Seminary Ridge and began his descent down the slope. "As he passed me," writes Longstreet, "he rode gracefully, with his jaunty cap racked well over his right ear and his long auburn locks, nicely dressed, hanging almost to his shoulders. He seemed a holiday soldier." Echo repeats the words: A holiday soldier! A holiday soldier!

There Now!

Even General Lee was unfair to our troops, and General Long, his biographer, in more than one place misapprehended the facts. In reply to a letter from this writer he promised to make a correction if a second edition of his large and interesting biography was called for.

We refer to the third day at Gettysburg so soon again because of a letter that reached us on Monday postmarked "Charleston, S. C, April 9." It comes from a soldier who did not belong to either Pettigrew's or Pickett's command. He writes, and he is clearly a man of education and fairness:

"I am glad to see you are taking up the claim of Pettigrew's brigade to share in the glory of Gettysburg. Why not go a little further? Pettigrew led his division. Pickett did not. Pettigrew was wounded, and no member of his staff came out of the fight without being wounded or having his horse shot under him. Neither Pickett nor any member of his staff nor even one of the horses was touched. Why? Because dismounted and on the farther side of a hill that protected them from the enemy's fire." There is in this city a letter from a distinguished, able, scholarly Virginian that states General Pickett was not in the charge at all. There now! The correspondent adds: "Investigate the statement, and if correct, this will help to make history somewhat truthful." He gives excellent authority — a gallant citizen of Savannah, Ga., who was in the battle and of whom we have known for more than thirty-three years. Let the whole truth come out as to the splendid charge on the third day, who participated in and who went farthest in and close to the enemy. — *Wilmington Messenger*.

Gov. Kemper Killed in Battle and Other Matters

The following extract is taken from a magazine article written by Mr. J. F. Rhodes in 1899: "Then the union guns reopened. When near enough canister shot was added, 'the slaughter was terrible.' The Confederate artillery reopened over the heads of the charging column trying to divert the fire of the union cannon, but it did not change the aim of the batteries from the charging column. When near enough the Federal infantry opened, but on swept the devoted division. Near the Federal lines Pickett made a pause 'to close ranks and mass for a final plunge.' Armistead leaped the stonewall and cried, 'Give them the cold steel, boys' laid his hand on a Federal gun, and the next moment was killed. At the same time Garnett and Kemper, Pickett's other brigadiers, were killed. Hill's corps wavered, broke ranks and fell back. 'The Federals swarmed around Pickett,' writes Longstreet, 'attacking on all sides, enveloped and broke up his command. They drove the fragments back upon our lines. Pickett gave the word to retreat.'"

To give a clear idea of the closing events of this assault it will be well to mention several things not generally known. Just at the point which had been occupied, but was then abandoned by Webb's brigade, there was no stonewall, but a breastwork made of rails covered with a little earth. Those works jutted out into the field. On both sides of this salient there were stonewalls. Of the one thousand men who reached these works of rails and earth only about fifty followed Armistead to the abandoned guns. The others stopped there. Seeing this all to their right, more than half the column did the same, and having stopped they were obliged to lie down. The left of the line continued to move on for a while when they, to prevent annihilation, also fell to the ground. This discontinuance of the forward movement, showing that the momentum of the charge had spent itself, meant defeat. Our men knew this, but there they lay waiting for — they knew not what. All other things that happened — the capture of men, muskets and flags — were for the Federals, mere details in reaping the harvest of victory.

Safe Surrender or Dangerous Retreat?

Leaving out Lane's brigade, which lay far over to the left in the Emmittsburg Road, our line, which was so imposing at the beginning of the assault, covered the front of only two Federal brigades at its close. Into the interval between Lane's and Pettigrew's troops New Yorkers were sent, who attacked the left of the latter's own brigade. About the same time Vermonters moved up and fired several volleys into Pickett's right. Which body of these flankers first made their attack has been a subject of some dispute, but it is a matter of no importance. Neither attack was made before Armistead was wounded. But there is a matter of very great importance, and that is to correctly decide which of the two contrary lines of action taken that day is the more honorable and soldier-like. Here were troops lying out in the open field, all of them knowing that they had met with a frightful defeat. Those on the left, seeing a move on the part of the enemy to effect their capture, though it a duty they owed themselves, their army and their country to risk their lives in an effort to escape. Acting upon this thought they went to the rear with a rush, helter skelter, devil take the hindmost, and the most of them did escape. Those on the right when ordered to surrender did so almost to a man. The North Carolinians, Alabamians and Tennesseeans upon the field felt that to surrender when there was a reasonable hope of escape was very little better than desertion. If the opinions of the Virginians were not quite as extreme as this, they certainly would have been surprised at that time had they been told that their conduct was heroic. Since then maudlin sentimentalists have so often informed them it was that now they believe it. The time may come when history will call their surrender by its right name.

Stragglers

The late Gen. James Dearing, of Virginia, at the time of the battle an artillery major, witnessed the assault, and shortly afterwards, giving a description of it to a friend of the writer, mentioned a circumstance which partly accounts for the fact that all of Pickett's troops were not captured. It was that from the very start individuals began to drop out of ranks, and that the number of these stragglers continued to increase as the line advanced, and that before a shot had ever been fired at them it amounted to many hundreds. This conduct on the part of so many must be taken into consideration in accounting for the shortness of our line at the close of the assault; also that the troops both to the right and left dressing upon Archer's brigade there was in consequence much crowding towards the centre. By adding to these causes the deaths and wounds the explanation of a condition which has puzzled many writers is readily seen.

"The Post Of Death And Honor"

General Longstreet is supposed to have always thought that after the second of Pettigrew's brigades gave way there were none of Hill's troops left upon the field. This General, while honest, was so largely imaginative that his statement of facts is rarely worthy of credence. He says that "Pickett gave the word to retreat." There are very many old soldiers, many even in Richmond, who do not believe that Pickett was there to give that word. That in the beautiful language of a recent writer, "He may have been trying to reach the post of death and honor, but he was far away, and valor could not annihilate space."

Judging Others By Ourselves

Gen. Longstreet is reported recently to have said at Gettysburg that if Gen. Meade had advanced his whole line on July 4th he would have carried everything before him. It is hardly fair for Gen. Longstreet to do so, but he is evidently judging the army by his troops, some of whom are said to have been so nervous and shaky after this battle that the crack of a teamster's whip would startle them. He is mistaken, for it must be remembered that the enemy was about as badly battered as we were, and that the troops composing Ewell's and Hill's Corps had beaten this enemy only two months before when it was on the defensive. Now we would have been on the defensive; is it probable that we would have been beaten?

Pettigrew's Brigade

This brigade was composed of the 11th, 26th, 47th, 52nd and 44th North Carolina. When the army went on the Gettysburg campaign the last named regiment was left in Virginia. That this brigade had more men killed and wounded at Gettysburg than any brigade in our army ever had in any battle is not so much to its credit as is the fact that after such appalling losses it was one of the two brigades selected for the rear guard when the army recrossed the river. At Gettysburg Capt. Tuttle's company of the 26th Regiment went into the battle with three officers and eighty-four men. All the officers and eighty-three of the men were killed or wounded. In the same battle company C of the 11th Regiment, had two officers killed (First Lieut. Tom Cooper, a University boy, was one of them) and thirty-four out of the thirty-eight men killed or wounded. Capt. Bird with the four remaining men participated in the assault of the third day, and of them the flag-bearer was shot and the captain brought out the colors himself. He was made major, and was afterwards killed at Reams Station. Bertie County should raise a monument to his memory. In the assault Col. Marshall, of the 52nd, commanded this brigade 'till he was killed. At the close of the battle Maj. Jones, of the 26th, was the only field officer who had not been struck, and he was subsequently killed at the Wilderness.

Desertion

With the exception of South Carolina probably no state in the Confederacy had so few soldiers "absent without leave" as North Carolina. Owing to unfortunate surroundings neither the head of the army nor the administration ever realized this fact. The same harshness that forced thousands of conscripts into the army who were unfit for service, and kept them there until death in the hospital released them, caused more soldiers from North Carolina (some of whom had shed their blood in defence of the South) to be shot for this so-called desertion than from any other state. Though the military population of the Tar Heel State was not as great as that of at least two of the others, her soldiers filled twice as many graves, and at Appomattox, Va., and Greensboro, N.C., surrendered twice as many muskets as those of any other state. There was a singular fact in connection with these so-called desertions. In summer, when there was fighting or the expectation of a fight, they never occurred. Only in winter, when the men had time to think of their families, hundreds of whom were suffering for the necessaries of life, did the longing desire to see them and minister to their wants overcome every other sentiment, and dozens of them would steal away.

Undeserved Contempt

Wonder and surprise must be felt by any intelligent officer of any of the European armies who rides over that part of the lines held by the army of the Potomac which was assaulted on the afternoon of July 3rd, 1863. Wonder that sixty or seventy thousand men occupying the commanding position did and supported by hundreds of cannon should have felt so much pride in having defeated a column of less than ten thousand. For had their only weapons been brick-bats they should have done so. Surprise that Gen. Lee should have had so supreme a contempt for the Federal army as to have thought for a moment that by any sort of possibility the attack could be successful.

A Leaf of Northern History

No longer ago than last August a New York magazine contained an elaborately illustrated article descriptive of the Gettysburg battlefield. As long as the writer confines himself to natural scenery he acquits himself very creditably, but when he attempts to describe events which occurred there so many years ago he flounders fearfully. Of course Pickett's men advance "alone." Of course there is a terrific hand-to-hand battle at what he calls the "bloody angle." In this battle he says that many of Doubleday's troops lost from twenty-five to forty percent. "The slaughter of the Confederates was fearful — nearly one half of them were left upon the field, Garnett's brigade alone having over three thousand killed and captured." This is Northern history.

Now for facts: Pickett's men did not advance "alone." There was no terrific battle inside the enemy's works. None of Doubleday's troops lost there from twenty-five to forty percent. There was not one regiment in Gibbons' or Doubleday's commands which, after the shelling, lost one-fourth of one percent. As to Garnett's brigade, as it carried in only two thousand or less and brought out a considerable fragment, it could hardly have had over three thousand killed and captured. It did have seventy-eight killed and three hundred and twenty-four wounded.

Gen. Doubleday in writing to ask permission to make use of the pamphlet in a history he was then preparing, suggested only one alteration, and that was in regard to Stannard's Vermont brigade, which had fought only the day before, and not the two days as the pamphlet had it.

Union Sentiment In North Carolina

On the retreat Kilpatrick attacked our ambulance train and captured many wounded officers of Ewell's corps. Among them was one from my brigade who, when in hospital, was asked by a Federal surgeon if the well-known Union sentiment in North Carolina had anything to do with the large proportion of wounded men from that State. Being young and inexperienced in the ways of the world he indignantly answered, "No."

Humbuggery of History

Early in the war the best troops in the Army of Northern Virginia could not have fighting enough. At that time they were simple enough to believe that there was some connection between fame and bravery. After a while they learned that a dapper little clerk of the quartermaster's department, if he had the ear of the editor of the *Richmond Examiner*, had more to do with their reputation than their own courage. When this fact became known there was "no more spoiling for a fight," but it was very often felt to be a hardship when they were called upon to do more than their proper share of fighting.

Brockenborough's Virginia Brigade

The 40th, 47th and 55th Virginia regiments and 22nd Virginia battalion composed this brigade. Up to the reorganization of the army after Jackson's death, it formed a part of A. P. Hill's famous light division. That it did not sustain its reputation at Gettysburg had no effect upon the general result of that battle. Their loss was 25 killed and 143 wounded.

Longstreet's Men

If any searcher after the truth of the matter consults the records and other sources of reliable information, paying no attention to the clap-traps of Virginia writers, he will find, to say the least, that the troops of Ewell's and Hill's Corps were the peers of the best and the superiors of a large part of the soldiers of Longstreet's corps. In the battle of the second day if the four brigades of McLaw's division had fought as well as did Wright's and Wilcox's of the third corps, we would have undoubtedly gained a victory at Gettysburg. Hood's was the best division, but it was defeated at Wauhatchie, Tenn., by troops that the men of the second and third corps had often met and never failed to drive. As to Pickett's "writing division:" From Malvern Hill to Gettysburg was exactly one year, and in this time the four great battles of Second Manassas, Sharpsburg, Fredericksburg and Chancellorsville, and twice as many of less prominence were fought by the army or parts of the army. In these battles Lane's North Carolina, Scales' North Carolina and Archer's mixed brigade of Tennesseeans and Alabamians had three thousand six hundred and ten men killed and wounded. In the same period Armistead's Virginia, Kemper's Virginia and Garnett's Virginia had seven hundred and seventy-two killed and wounded.

Scales' Brigade

At Gettysburg where it had 102 killed and 322 wounded it was a small brigade, as at Chancellorsville only two months before it had met with a loss of nearly seven hundred. In the third; day's assault, General Scales having been wounded, it was commanded by Col. Lowrence, who was also wounded as was every field officer and nearly every company officer in the brigade. This gallant little organization consisted of the 13th, 16th, 22nd, 34th and 38th North Carolina. Its first commander was Pettigrew, who was severely wounded and captured at Seven Pines. Then came Pender, then Scales, late governor of North Carolina. At Gettysburg it and Lane's were the only troops who were required to fight every day.

Mr. W. H. Swallow, of Maryland, a Confederate soldier and a

writer of some note, was wounded at Gettysburg, and in one of his articles descriptive of the battle, says: "Gen. Trimble, who commanded Pender's division and lost a leg in the assault, lay wounded with the writer at Gettysburg for several weeks after the battle, related the fact to the writer (Swallow) that when (Gen. Lee was inspecting the column in front of Scales' brigade, which had been fearfully cut up in the first day's conflict, having lost very heavily, including all of its regimental officers with its gallant commander, and noticing many of Scales' men with their heads and hands bandaged, he said to Gen. Trimble: 'Many of these poor boys should go to the rear; they are not able for duty.' Passing his eyes searchingly along the weakened ranks of Scales' brigade he turned to Gen. Trimble and touchingly added, 'I miss in this brigade the faces of many dear friends.'"

In a few weeks some of us were removed from the town to a grove near the wall that Longstreet had assaulted. As the ambulances passed the fences on the Emmittsburg Road, the slabs were so completely perforated with bullet holes that you could scarcely place a half inch between them. One inch and a quarter board was indeed a curiosity. It was sixteen feet long and fourteen inches wide and was perforated with eight hundred and thirty-six musket balls. I learned afterwards that the board was taken possession of by an agent of the Pennsylvania Historical Society. This board was on that part of the fence where Scales' brave little brigade crossed it.

Steuart's Brigade

This brigade was composed of the 10th, 23rd and 37th Virginia, the Maryland battalion and the 1st and 3rd North Carolina. When Gen. Ed Johnson, supported by two of Rodes' brigades, made his attack on the morning of the third day, this brigade displayed conspicuous gallantry. Had Gen. Longstreet moved forward at the same time, the story of Gettysburg might have been written very differently. There was not an indifferent company in this brigade. All were choice troops. The 3rd North Carolina possessed in a pre-eminent degree the mental obtuseness peculiar to so many North Carolina troops. Try as they would, they never could master the art of assaulting entrenchments or fighting all day in an open field without having somebody hurt. In the Sharpsburg campaign it had more men killed and wounded than any regiment in the army. At Chancellorsville there were only three — all North Carolina — whose casualties were greater, and at Gettysburg (losing fifty percent) it headed the list for its division. The 1st North Carolina, a somewhat smaller regiment, in number of casualties always followed close behind the Third, except at Mechanicsville, when it went far ahead. It was indeed also one of those fool regiments which could never learn the all-important lesson which so many of their more brilliant comrades found no difficulty in acquiring.

Col. Fox in his *Regimental Losses*, says: "To all this some may sneer and some may say, '*Cui Bono?*' If so let it be remembered that there are other reasons than money or patriotism which induce men to risk life and limb in war. There is the love of glory and the expectation of honorable recognition; but the private in the ranks expects neither; his identity is merged in that of his regiment; to him the regiment and its name is everything; he does not expect to see his own name appear upon the page of history, and is content with the proper recognition of the old command in which he fought. But he is jealous of the record of his regiment and demands credit for every shot it faced and every grave it filled. The bloody laurels for which a regiment contends will always be awarded to the one with the longest roll of honor. Scars are the true evidence of wounds, and regimental scars can be seen only in its record of casualties."

Defeat With Honor

How much punishment must a body of troops receive before they can, without discredit to themselves, confess that they have been defeated? In answer it may be stated that in front of Marye's Hill at Fredericksburg, Maegher's and Zook's brigades lost in killed and wounded, respectively, thirty-six and twenty-six percent, and that the killed and wounded of the fifteen Pennsylvania regiments, constituting Meade's division, which broke through Jackson's line, was 36 percent. This division was not only repulsed but routed, and yet they were deservedly considered amongst the very best troops in their army. Ordinarily it may be safely said that a loss of twenty-five percent, satisfies all the requirements of military honor. Ordinarily is said advisedly, for in our army very much depended upon knowing from what State the regiment or brigade hailed before it could be decided whether or not it was justified in retreating. When on the afternoon of the third day of July, 1863, Pettigrew's, Trimble's and Pickett's divisions marched into that ever-to-be remembered slaughter pen, there was one regiment in the first named division, the 11th Mississippi, which entered the assault fresh, carrying in 325 officers and men. After losing 202 killed and wounded, it with its brigade, left the field in disorder. Correspondents of Virginia newspapers witnessing their defeat accused them of bad behavior. Virginian historians repeated their story and the slander of brave men, who had lost sixty percent before retreating, lives to this day. In the spring of 1862 an army, consisting of ten regiments of infantry, one of calvary and two batteries of artillery, was defeated in the valley and the loss in killed and wounded was four hundred and fifty-five. In the summer of 1863 there were eight regiments in the same division who took part in a certain battle and were defeated; but they did not confess themselves beaten 'till the number of their killed and wounded amounted to two thousand and two (2,002) — a loss so great that it never was before or afterwards equalled in our army or in any American army. In the first instance all of the troops were from Virginia and as consolation for their defeat they received a vote of thanks from the Confederate Congress. In the second case five of the regiments were from North Carolina and three from Mississippi. Did our Congress thank them for such unprecedented display of endurance? No indeed! Corrupted as it was by Richmond flattery and dominated by Virginian opinion; the only wonder is that it refrained from a vote of censure.

Western Army

Four North Carolina infantry regiments, 29th, 39th, 58th and 60th, and one of cavalry, served in the Western army and did so with credit to themselves and State.

Cook's Brigade

The 15th, 27th, 46th and 48th regiments composed this brigade. It met with its greatest losses at Sharpsburg, Fredericksburg, Bristoe Station and the Wilderness. The 15th, while in Cobb's brigade, suffered great loss at Malvern Hill in addition to above. The 48th fought at Oak Grove June 25th the first of the seven days' battles, and suffered severely. The 27th was probably more praised for its conduct at Sharpsburg than any regiment in the army.

Ransom's Brigade

The 24th, 25th, 35th, 49th and 56th made up this brigade. It probably met with its greatest loss at Malvern Hill. The 24th of this brigade and the 14th of Geo. B. Anderson's both claim that after this battle their dead were found nearest to where the enemy's artillery had stood. The brigade also displayed conspicuous gallantry at Sharpsburg, Fredericksburg and Drury's Bluff.

Junior Reserves

Gov. Vance called them his "seed wheat." There were four regiments and one battalion of these troops. They were used for the most part to guard bridges from raiders, but a large part of them fought at Wise's Fork, below Kinston, and at Bentonville, where they acquitted themselves creditably. A witness has told the writer of having seen one of these children who a few days before had lost both eyes by a musket ball. He said it was the "saddest sight of a sad, sad war."

"Red Leg" Infantry

After the fall of Fort Fisher several battalions of heavy artillery which had been occupying the other forts near the mouth of the Cape Fear, were withdrawn and armed as infantry, joined Johnston's army. No troops ever fought better than they did at Kinston and Bentonville. At the latter battle one of these battalions was commanded by Lt. Col. Jno. D. Taylor, who lost an arm on that occasion.

The Critics

While the notices of the pamphlet have been generally favorable, it was not to be expected that all would be so. There are those who see no need for reopening the question herein discussed. While confessing that a part of our troops have been directly wronged by slanderous words and all them wronged by implication, they assert that time only is required to make all things even, and that the dead past should be allowed to bury its dead. Peace loving souls they deprecate controversy, believing that from it will result only needless heart burnings.

Then again there are others who object not only to the tone and temper of the article, but to the mere statement of indisputable facts. There should be, they say, a feeling of true comradeship among all who have served in the same army, especially in such an army as ours. That comrades should assist and defend each other in person and reputation, and under no circumstances should anything be done or said to wound or offend. To admit that there has been provocation in one direction does not justify provocation in another, for two wrongs never yet made a right. That to write of anything to the discredit of a part of the Army of Northern Virginia is to a certain extent to injure the reputation of the whole army, and that a sentiment of loyalty to that army and love for its head should prompt its veterans to place its honor above all other considerations. Some old soldiers within and some without the limits of the State have expressed these opinions. Many others may entertain them. It may be they are right. It may be they are wrong. Who can tell? However, letters never printed show that there are many who think when once an effort in behalf of justice is begun it should be continued 'till that end is attained, and be it remembered that the justice demanded is for the dead who cannot defend themselves.

Kirkland's Brigade

The 17th, 42nd, 50th and 66th North Carolina composed this brigade, and it was first commanded by Gen. Jas. Martin. It was not sent to Virginia 'till the spring of 1864, when it was placed in a division made up for Gen. Hoke. It was hotly engaged in the battle of Drury's Bluff where Lt. Col. Lamb, of the 17th, was mortally wounded, at Cold Harbor where Col. Moore, the boy commander of the 66th, was killed, at Bentonville, Kinston, etc. But it is probable that the hardships endured in the trenches at Petersburg were responsible for more deaths than all the bullets of the enemy.

Artillery

Seven North Carolina batteries served in Virginia. All of them were very efficient, but three of them were so remarkably fine that it is a temptation to name them.

Cavalry

We had five regiments and one battalion of cavalry to serve in Virginia. They were the 9th, 19th, 41st, 59th and 63rd North Carolina troops; but generally known as 1st, 2nd, 3rd, 4th and 5th cavalry and the 16th battalion. If space permitted, incidents worth mentioning connected with each of these organizations could be told. As it is, only two, which may interest North Carolinians generally, and citizens of Halifax County in particular, will be mentioned. In the summer of 1864 when General Butler came so near capturing Petersburg, at that time defenseless, the 16th North Carolina battalion was picketing the road by which the Federals were approaching. It was then that this battalion, assisted by two light field guns, acted with so much spirit that the advance of Butler's men was so delayed that time was given for troops from Lee's army to arrive and man the fortifications. Prominent among the heroes on this occasion was a Halifax boy — Lt. W. F. Parker. On the disastrous field of Five Forks our cavalry was not only holding its own, but was driving that of the enemy when the infantry gave way. This success of the cavalry on their part of the line was very nearly the last ever gained by any portion of our army. They had been fighting by squadrons and that composed of the Onslow and Halifax companies of the 3rd regiment had just made a successful charge, when, looking to the left, they saw the infantry retreating in disorder. The squadron on this occasion was commanded and led by a Scotland Neck mounted rifleman, the late Norfleet Smith — a brave officer, a good citizen and a loyal friend. Dear old "Boots" of other days! Lightly lie the sod above your honored head.

"Earth has no such soldiers now, Such true friends are not found."

Thirty-sixth N. C. Troops

This was a heavy artillery regiment stationed at Fort Fisher when the final attack was made upon this fort. After the fire from the ships had dismounted their big guns and the assault by land was being made, they snatched up their muskets and showed the enemy how well they could use them. It is now generally conceded that not in the whole war did a body of soldiers ever struggle so long and so desperately against the inevitable. From traverse to traverse, from gun-chamber to gun-chamber for several hours the hopeless struggle went on. Capt. Hunter's Halifax company had 58 men killed and wounded out of 80 present. A letter from a gallant member of the company, says:

"There never was a formal surrender. It (the fort) was taken by piece-meal — that is, one gun-chamber at a time." When the capture of this place was announced in Richmond and before any of the facts regarding it were known, the abuse and vilification heaped upon its devoted garrison was something astonishing — even for that very censorious city.

Clingman's Brigade

This brigade was composed of the 8th, 31st, 51st and 61st North Carolina. It served in South Carolina a great part of the war, and for the gallant conduct of the 51st in the defense of Fort Wagner, this regiment was complimented in orders. The brigade took a prominent part in the brilliant capture of Plymouth. It was engaged at Goldsboro, Batchelor Creek — where Colonel Henry Shaw, of the 8th, was killed — and at other points in North Carolina, before it went to Virginia, which it did early in 1864. There it became a part of the command of Major General Hoke. After having heroically borne all the privations and dangers which fell to the lot of this "splendid division," as styled by General Joe Johnston, it surrendered with it at Greensboro.

Number of NC Troops

The compiler of our Roster adds up the number of names printed in the four volumes, and makes a total of 104,498; but to arrive at an approximation of the real number many subtractions, and very many more additions, will have to be made.

The First Volunteers was a six months regiment (twelve companies) and was disbanded when its term enlistment expired. All of its companies re-enlisted, and thus these men were counted twice, right of these companies, with the addition of two new ones, becoming the famous Eleventh regiment. Many officers were counted three, four, and sometimes five times in cases where they had been successively promoted. There were a great many transfers from one regiment to another, and in nearly every instance the individual transferred would be counted with both regiments. The Fourth cavalry battalion was incorporated in a regiment, and its 271 names are counted twice. The Seventh battalion (detailed artisans) contains the names of 402 men who were detailed from regiments in active service, and of course they were counted twice. All of these repetitions would probably reduce the number given by the compiler of the State Roster by 3,600 and make it about 100,900. On the other hand this number should probably be increased by 9,100. One entire regiment (the 68th), which carried upon its rolls at least 1,000 names, is not counted, for none of its rolls could be found. In many regiments the rolls printed were those in use the last year of the war, when they had been reduced to skeletons. For instance, in the 60th Regiment the rolls of only nine companies could be found, which carried upon them only 467 names. The surviving officers of the missing company getting together, made out a roll from memory embracing the whole war, and the number of names was 114. So it is certain that this regiment should have had more than twice as many names as it is credited with. The fighting 27th is only allowed 802 officers and men, when the 26th and 28th are both given considerably more than 1,800. The 37th is credited with 1,928 names, while the 54th has only 663. Both of these regiments served in the Army of Northern Virginia, and it is a fair presumption that they both received about the same number of conscripts. Basing his calculations upon our Roster, and some other sources of information, the writer has arrived at the conclusion that the number of soldiers furnished by North Carolina to the Confederacy was about 110,000. Of course hundreds of this number shortly after enlisting were discharged as unfit for service. Many more should have been discharged and were not, but were required to undergo hardships that they were physically unable to bear, and the consequence was that they died by thousands.

Of the number furnished, nineteen thousand six hundred and seventy-three are known to have been killed outright or died of wounds. Other thousands lost legs and arms, or were otherwise mutilated for life. Twenty thousand six hundred and two are known to have died of disease; and very many of these deaths are directly attributable either to the ignorance of our surgeons or the misdirected zeal that prompted them to retain in the service men who were unfit for its duties, many of them being little better than confirmed invalids.

The great statistician. Colonel Fox, says: "The phrase, 'Military population,' as used in the eighth census, represents the white males between the ages of 18 and 45, and included all who were unfit for military duty on account of physical or mental infirmities. These exempts — which include also all cases of minor defects — constitute in every country one-fifth of the military population." Taking one-fifth from our military population we should have furnished to the Confederate armies ninety-two thousand two hundred and ninety-seven soldiers. But as said above we did send to the front about one hundred and ten thousand, thirty-six percent, of whom died.

APPENDIX

East Las Vegas, N. M.

Enclosed please find 25¢ in stamps in payment for *Pettigrew's Charge*. I have read it with much interest. I think you have made a good case and that you are right. I was at Vicksburg the same day — the Adjt. 81st Ills. Vols. Infty.

I am yours truly,
J. J. Fitzgerald
Post Dept. Comd'r Dept. N. M. G. A. R.

Abbeville, S. C, July 1st, 1896.

Dear Sir: — I enclose 25¢ in stamps for which be kind enough to send me your pamphlet entitled, *Pickett or Pettigrew?* if you have any copies on hand. I recently saw a copy in Charleston. You agree with me about Pettigrew and Pickett. I was Sergt. Major of Orr's Rifles, McGowan's brigade, Wilcox's division. Some years ago I was looking at the cyclorama of Gettysburg in Philadelphia. The Yankee who explained the battle said that A. P. Hill's men advanced further than Pickett's, and pointed out to the crowd where a number of North Carolinians fell at the extreme front.

Yours truly,
Robt. R. Hemphill

"JUSTICE FOR OUR DEAD IS ALL WE WANT."

Washington, D. C, Dec. 29th, 1888

My Dear Sir: — Circumstances here have caused me to be so very busy of late that I have not had time sooner to acknowledge your courtesy in sending me the pamphlet on the battle of Gettysburg, I seize the occasion of the holidays to do so. The pamphlet was read by every member of my family with the keenest interest. I have to thank you from my heart for writing it. No living man suffers more from these mean and jealous attempts to deprive North Carolina of her proper honor than I do. I sometimes almost get sick over them. I have always regarded the effort of some Virginians, not all, thank God, to deprecate the North Carolina troops in the battle of Gettysburg as simply a damnable and dastardly outrage. But let us take courage. The simple truth will ultimately prevail — simple justice is all we want for our dead. Your friend and fellow North Carolinian.

[*The above was written by one who loved North Carolina and one whom North Carolina loved to honor.*]

A WISE JUDGE.

The following is an extract from a letter written by a resident of Chicago, Major Chas. A. Hale, who has the honor of having served in the Fifth New Hampshire, a regiment which fought gallantly at Gettysburg, and is distinguished for having sustained the greatest losses in battle of any infantry or cavalry regiment in the whole Union army:

"There is not a shadow of a doubt in my mind but that the sons of North Carolina, Tennessee and Mississippi carved on the tablets of history equal laurels with the sons of Virginia in the great events of that supreme attempt to gain victory on Cemetery Ridge. Pettigrew and Trimble deserve equal honors with Pickett, and if we weigh with judicial exactness more, for impartial evidence proves that they suffered in a greater degree, and forced their way nearer the lines where pitiless fate barred their entrance. The nearest point reached by any troops was Bryan's barn; this is made conclusive by evidence on both sides. If there were a thousand Confederates inside the stonewall at the angle more than two-thirds of that number must have been Pettigrew's men."

HOW PICKETT'S DIVISION 'ABSQUATULATED.'

Pickett's division of the Army of Northern Virginia is rarely heard of either before or after Gettysburg. No body of troops during the last war made as much reputation on so little fighting. Newspaper men did the work by printer's ink and the casualties were small.

Fourteen hundred and ninety-nine were captured at Gettysburg. More than this number "absquated" when Petersburg fell and there was a probability of leaving Virginia. Pickett's division made a poor show at the surrender at Appomattox. — Abbeville, (S. C.) *Medium*.

ÆSOP'S FABLE — THE DOG AND THE BONE.

"They digged a pit,
They digged it deep.
They digged it for their brothers ;
But it so fell out that they fell in
The pit that was digged for t'others."

An interesting contribution to the history of the battle of Gettysburg is afforded in a pamphlet essay entitled *Pickett or Pettigrew?* by Capt. W. R. Bond, a Confederate staff officer in the Army of Northern Virginia. Capt. Bond's desire is to correct the commonly received accounts of the parts taken in that battle by the troops commanded by Gens. Pickett and Pettigrew.

Gen. Longstreet, according to Capt. Bond, is largely responsible for the current misrepresentation of the Southern side of the story of Gettysburg, and he tells in detail a curious story of the favoritism displayed all through the war towards everything Virginian at the expense of the soldiers from the other Southern States.

— *Springfield Republican.*

We have read with much interest a pamphlet by Capt. W. R. Bond, entitled *Pickett or Pettigrew?* in which the writer, a North Carolinian, proposed to show, and does show very conclusively, that the losses of Pettigrew's North Carolina brigade in this charge were greater than those sustained by Pickett or, indeed, by any command in the army. He claims that the twenty-sixth regiment of this brigade suffered greater loss than that of any command in modern times. The fate of one company in this regiment recalls Thermopylae; it was literally wiped out — every man in it was either killed or wounded. This pamphlet makes a glorious showing for the resolute courage and intrepidity of the North Carolina troops, but it is endorsed by the brave boys here who fought by their side. It also pays a high tribute to the Tennesseeans engaged in that bloody fight, according them the place they occupied in it and the meed of praise they justly won.

— Gallatin (Tenn.) *Examiner.*

It contains some interesting statements from the Southern, and especially from North Carolina, point of view, the object of its author being to show that undue credit has been given to Pickett's Virginia brigades at the expense of the brigade of Pettigrew from North Carolina. The author contends that undue prominence has been given to the part taken by Virginia troops in the war of the rebellion, owing to the leading part taken by Virginia newspapers and Virginia historians in reporting the events of the war. He shows that North Carolina leads in the report given in Col. Fox's paper on the "Chances of Being Hit in Battle." Of the troops losing the most men Mississippi comes next, and Virginia does not appear at all. He has suggestive reference also to the possibility of Gen. Longstreet being of Gascon descent. Altogether, his little pamphlet is lively reading.

— *Army and Navy Journal.*

A review of this pamphlet ought to and shall be carefully written. His reference to Gen. Pettigrew is in admirable taste and will evoke new sorrow for the untimely death of that cultivated gentleman and splendid soldier; but the dedication to Hill's Corps is marred by a spirit which no provocation can justify. An author who loses his temper always breaks the force of his argument and weakens his cause. And so in the present case some salient facts which Capt. Bond presents lose most of their strength and effect by the spirit in which he clothes them.

And suppose the charge of Pickett was given undue prominence in the general history of the war, (and we do not dispute it), was it kind or proper on that account to make a systematic attempt to vitiate the record of all the service rendered by Virginia to the Confederate arms?

And it is a worthy duty to resurrect those brave deeds from oblivion, a duty which Capt. Bond is well competent to discharge, and in the discharge of which every Confederate Virginian would bid him "God speed." But he will pardon us for saying that the task, to serve any good purpose, must be approached in a different tone and temper than that displayed in his recent pamphlet, for we have passed by much of insinuation and allegation his work contains, hoping that a calmer frame of mind will lead the author to vindicate in another edition the name and fame of the gallant Carolinians without seeking to pluck one laurel from the wreath with which friend and foe have crowned the Virginia charge at Gettysburg.

— *Petersburg Index-Appeal.*

After an inexplicable silence of nearly twenty-five years, the North Carolinians are beginning to assert themselves in regard to the charge on the third day at Gettysburg. Every student of the history of the war knows that it was not Pickett, of Virginia, but Pettigrew, of North Carolina, who was entitled to the principal credit for the charge. Pickett started out in command of the charging column, but stopped when within half a mile of our line, while Pettigrew went on with his North Carolinians and reached the farthest point attained by any rebel troops. — *National Tribune.*

Hall and Sledge are the publishers of this remarkable pamphlet, which not only disparages Virginia and Virginia papers as they were during the War Between the States, but even Pickett's Virginians. The world has passed upon all these matters, and its verdict will not be changed. — *Richmond Dispatch.*

W. W. Owen, of New Orleans, late Lt. Colonel of Washington artillery, A. N. V., writes: "I have just seen a newspaper account of 'Pickett's charge,' by Capt. W. R. Bond, and am anxious to obtain a copy. I was at the battle of Gettysburg and I think his account of it will agree with my idea about it, at least as far as Pickett was concerned." This little book is well written and the author corrects a number of errors which have been published about certain battles of the late unpleasantness. It is worth reading — *Tallahassee Floridian.*

The *Wilmington Star* noticing an article in the *Richmond Times*:

"We see from the *Richmond Times* that a reply is preparing to Captain W. R. Bond's stinging pamphlet on the battle of Gettysburg. The Virginians do not intend to have it go down to history that North Carolinians did as well at Gettysburg, or better, than the much trumpeted division of Pickett. North Carolinians must see to it that the brave men who made such a splendid record at Gettysburg are neither defamed nor robbed.

T. Blyler, Captain in the 12th New Jersey, writes: "Your division (meaning Pettigrew's) advanced in our front and we bear willing testimony to your bravery and to penetrating farther than Pickett."

W. H. Shaver, of Kingston, Pa., who belonged to the Philadelphia brigade, writes: "If convenient, say to Capt. Bond that I have read his pamphlet with very great interest as well as astonishment, for we of the North know of no other soldiers in the charge but 'Pickett and his Virginians.' It is a well written article and will cause history to be re-written."

J. D. Yautier, of Philadelphia, historian of the 88th Regiment of Penn. Vols., writes: "I think it an excellent treatise, it appears to be the impression that the Virginians did about all the fighting on the Southern side during the war. To be a Virginian was to be all that was good. The record shows that the North Carolinians were away up head."

W. E. Potter, Colonel of the 12th New Jersey, writes: "In an address delivered by myself at Gettysburg May, 1886, I called attention to the gallant conduct of the North Carolina troops and the extent of their losses when compared with Pickett's. So far as I know my speech was the first publication to point out the fact that the troops of Pickett constituted the minor portion of the assaulting column."

Col. George Meade, of Philadelphia, the son of Gen. Meade, who commanded the Federal forces in this battle, writes: "I am glad to find in it certain facts that confirm what has been my own impression as to the important part taken by the North Carolina troops in the assault at Gettysburg on the afternoon of the 3rd of July. I must congratulate you on having presented your case so strongly."

Captain W. R. Bond, a North Carolinian and a Confederate soldier, who agrees with Col. Batchelder, of Massachusetts, the Government historian of the battle of Gettysburg, that the brilliant military exploit popularly known as 'Pickett's charge' should be called 'Longstreet's assault,' has written a pamphlet to call attention to the fact that Pettigrew's Division of North Carolina troops in this charge went further and stayed longer and had more men killed than Pickett's

Division of Virginians. Captain Bond presents some interesting statements in the course of his narrative.

It may be added that the North Carolinians also lost, by "one of the frequent mischances that govern the direction of popular praise, their share of the glory that their bravery should have gained, and which Pickett's Division gathered for itself. — *Philadelphia Press.*

GEN. ULYSSES DOUBLEDAY.

Capt. Bond's pamphlet showing that Pettigrew and not Pickett is entitled to the glory that graced the Confederate banners at the battle of Gettysburg, is bearing fruit. It is bound to convince any fair-minded man who will read it. A private letter to the author from Asheville, says that the writer had a long conversation with Gen. Doubleday, a Federal officer and brother of the Gen. Doubleday mentioned in the pamphlet. "Gen. Doubleday contended," continues the letter, "that Pickett's men did as so-called history says they did, and reaped all the glory." I asked him as a personal favor to read the essay, *Pickett or Pettigrew?* He has just finished telling his opinion. Said he: "it opened my eyes. Your brave men have been slandered. Capt. Bond gives chapter and verse, it is a fine essay." — *Weldon News.*

Mr. O. W. Blacknall, of Kittrell, in a letter to the *News and Observer* concerning the ceremonies at Winchester last Friday, pays a high compliment to it. W. R. Bond's book, *Pickett or Pettigrew.* Mr. Blacknall mentions Capt. Bond's book as being one of the documents placed in the pocket of the cornerstone, and adds: "I will say in passing that the scholarly and profound brochure of Capt. Bond's — *Pickett or Pettigrew* — has never received the acknowledgment so eminently its due. Therein he clearly shows the manner in which history was shaped to North Carolina's detriment. The Richmond papers seeking to please their patrons, chiefly Virginians, to put it mildly, laid great stress on the services of Virginia troops and little on their failures. They killed and made alive reputations of men as they saw fit. Pollard and other historians writing from the Southern standpoint followed largely the Richmond papers, and thus history was miswritten to our apparently irretrievable harm. Captain Bond's pamphlet should be widely read and its substance preserved in history."
— *Scotland Neck Commonwealth.*

LONGSTREET AND N. C. SOLDIERS.

We copy a brief communication that will serve as an eye-opener to Longstreet's real claim upon North Carolina sympathizers. Our correspondent writes:

"There are some old soldiers from North Carolina, who have always liked and admired Gen. Longstreet and they regret to see the strictures upon him in a recently published pamphlet. If they will read carefully the following facts from the official records relating to the Sharpsburg campaign, they may feel that their partiality has been misplaced.

"General Longstreet had in this campaign nine North Carolina regiments, whose killed and wounded averaged one hundred and four. In his corps there were eighty regiments from other states and their average was sixty-four. In the eighty there were twenty-two Virginia regiments and their average was thirty-two. The 48th North Carolina had more men killed and wounded than any regiment of its corps. The 3rd North Carolina, of Jackson's corps, had more men killed and wounded than any regiment in the army. In fact, more than the entire brigades of Generals Armistead and Garnett combined. At the conclusion of his report of the operations of this campaign, General Longstreet mentions the names of thirty-eight officers, who had distinguished themselves for gallantry. In this number there is not one brigade or regiment commander from North Carolina."

— *Messenger.*

REGIMENTAL LOSSES.

A study of regimental actions shows clearly that the battalions which faced musketry the steadiest, the longest and the oftenest, were the ones whose aggregate loss during the war was greatest. Fighting regiments leave a bloody wake behind them; retreating regiments lose few men. At Chancellorsville the heaviest losses were in the corps that stood — not in the one that broke. — Fox.

W. K. B., in *Wilmington Messenger*:

I write you a letter, as I wish to tell you about certain conversations I lately had with an old Confederate — an officer of high rank, and one who, after the war, was on intimate terms with General Lee.

It will also contain a copy of a letter received by me some two months ago from a member of General Lee's staff, and some other things which I think will interest your old soldier readers. In one of the conversations referred to mention was made of the letters of General Cobb (who was killed at Fredericksburg) which have lately been published. In one of these letters General Cobb says that Mr. Davis and General Lee thought there was only one state in the Confederacy, and that was Virginia. In referring to it I remarked that, allowing a little for exaggeration, I did not think he was very far wrong; that I supposed it was much the same in the other states, and that I knew of the persistent injustice, and sometimes even cruelty, with which North Carolina and her troops were treated. He at once came to the defence of General Lee, and said he knew positively that he was not responsible for much of the injustice of which I complained; that in the matter of appointing and promoting officers General Lee often had very little influence. For instance, after Jackson's death, when the army was re-organized and the two corps made into three, he was bitterly opposed to having A. P. Hill and Ewell for corps commanders. He wished to have Rode — an Alabamian — to command one of them, and also wished to give a division to Pettigrew and he always said if his divisions and corps had been commanded at Gettysburg by officers of his choice he would have gained that battle. But, said General, as the secretary of war was a Virginian, and the influence of Virginia politicians was so all-powerful, both in the executive mansion and the halls of our congress, his wishes were not considered. Though a Virginian, he spoke at length of this baneful influence which festered for four years in Richmond. And just here it may be remarked that probably the most humiliating thing connected with our struggle for independence — more humiliating even than defeat — was the fact that North Carolinians and other free born men should ever have allowed themselves to be at all dominated by a public opinion, which was made by a sorry lot of ignoble bomb-proof hunters. On one occasion I told General about the letter I had received from Col. Venable, and how he happened to write it. That I had heard reports as to General Pickett, while the assault was being made, which reflected upon his courage, and was disposed to doubt them, as I had heard that he had acted very bravely in his vain attempt to rally his division when routed at Five Forks. I do not think I succeeded in convincing him of this, for I think he believes yet that General Pickett never went near his troops on this the day of their last battle.

Wishing to know if there were any grounds for these reports, I wrote to Colonel Venable, asking him how far into the field General Pickett advanced with his division, and how near he was to it when it was repulsed, and the following is his answer:

Remington, Fauquier County, Va.

"Dear Sir: — It has been settled by officers of the United States army, that both Pettigrew's and Pickett's men went to high water mark — that is, equally far in the charge at Gettysburg. The Federal government has caused marks to be placed at different points on the field with great care.

"The charge should even be called the charge of Pettigrew's and Pickett's men.

    Yours respectfully.
    Chas S. Venable.

"General Pettigrew was every inch a soldier and a very great loss to the grand old army of northern Virginia. C. S. V."

It will be seen that no attention is paid to my question, as there is no connection between it and the intended answer. This may signify something or it may not. My letter may have been mislaid and contents forgotten. The time has been when the reception of this letter would have greatly gratified me, but since I have made a study of the records and other authorities I have become convinced that, with one exception, there was not a brigade in Trimble's or Pettigrew's divisions which did not only equal but really surpass any of General Pickett's in all soldierly qualities on that occasion.

And now for a few of the figures you some time ago expressed the wish to see. For the whole battle the fifteen Virginia regiments on the right had in killed and wounded 1,360. Amongst those on the left were the five North Carolina and three Mississippi regiments, which constituted Pettigrew's and Davis' brigades, and their loss in killed and wounded was 2,002.

What part of this latter loss was incurred on the third day will never be accurately known; but we know from the Federals that the artillery fire was largely concentrated upon these two brigades, and we also know from the testimony of Federal officers, one of whom was Colonel Morgan, General Hancock's chief of staff, that the dead lay thicker on the ground over which these troops had passed than upon any other part of the field, and if we did not know these two facts the case of one regiment furnishes a key to the percentage of killed and wounded in its own brigade and that of the one immediately on its right. This regiment, the Eleventh Mississippi, did no fighting on the first day, as it was on detached service and consequently met with all its loss in the fight of the third. We know how many it carried in, and Dr. Guild's report informs us of the loss, and, knowing these numbers, we know that its percentage of killed and wounded was more than sixty — a percentage so high that not one Virginia regiment ever made it, and not a great many others. This and its companion regiment — the Second Mississippi — were old troops — veterans in fact as well as in name — had fought often and always well. By referring to the Sharpsburg Campaign Series 1. Vol. xix. of the records, a comparison can be readily drawn between the conduct of these two regiments in this campaign and that of several which were afterwards at Gettysburg with Pickett. A comparison that were it not so pitiful would be amusing.

If Pickett's troops carried in no more than claimed their percentage of killed and wounded was twenty-eight. But in order that their percentage might appear as high as possible, it is probable their numbers were always represented as smaller than they were. Their fifteen regiments probably averaged 400. If they did not, they should have done so, for they did not often have anybody hurt — that is, compared with the troops in the army from the other states. In the period from the close of the Richmond fighting to Gettysburg — one year — twelve battles were fought by the whole or part of the army, and in these battles Archer's Tennessee, Lane's North Carolina and Scales' North Carolina had 3,610 killed and wounded. Kemper's Virginia, Armistead's Virginia and Garnett's Virginia had 772. We can understand why these people were handled so tenderly, for were they not made of better clay than the fighters of the army? Fine porcelain from the province of Quang Tong were they — things of beauty, but fragile.

In the assault Davis' brigade had about sixty percent, killed and wounded. It is probable that Pettigrew's brigade had even a higher percentage, as they were somewhat longer under fire. It is possible that Pickett's was twenty-five. But whatever it was, after all, their pretty wheelings and lovely drum major's airs, that the enemy should have been so ungrateful as to shoot at them, so wounded their feelings that they had to be sent out of the army and they did not re-join it for nearly a year afterwards.

If a line of good soldiers can be formed in rushing distance, almost anything can be carried. But if a wide and open field has to be passed and there is to be a loss from twenty-five to seventy percent, and the consequent disorganization, nothing but useless bloodshed can be expected. This would appear to be a truth so self-evident that the merest tyro could comprehend it. But yet Burnside and Hancock (till too late) do not appear to have done so at Fredericksburg. General Lee did not at Malvern Hill and Gettysburg, and, in ignorance of this law, the gallant Schobelef sacrificed the best division of the Russian army at Plevna.

Bodies in motion, by their momentum, advance in the direction of least resistance. A body of soldiers making an attack forms no exception to this law of physics. When the Philadelphia brigade of Gibbon's division, which had been roughly handled the day before, gave way as our men got in charging distance, this point of least resistance was filled by Confederates — a disorganized mob of about 1,000 — in which several brigades had representatives, and this is very foolishly called the "high water mark of the Confederacy." Why, there was not a fresh regiment in the Federal army which could not have defeated this body, and there was a whole corps of fresh regiments at hand. The Sixth, which by many was considered the best in the army had hardly fired a shot. If there was any high water mark connected with this battle it was reached the afternoon before, while McLaws, Hood and Anderson were doing their fighting — and the precise time was when Wright's brigade, of the last named division, having driven the enemy before them, had carried a battery of twenty guns. Shortly afterwards one of McLaws' brigades gave way, and with its defeat went our fortunes. Every shot fired by us the next day was one more nail in the coffin of the Confederacy.

— *Scotland Neck Commonwealth.*

General George Edward Pickett

Other publications from

The Scuppernong Press

Lincoln As The South Should Know Him
.... O.W. Blacknall

Truth of the War Conspiracy of 1861
....H. W. Johnstone

A Story Behind Every Stone
....Charles E. Purser

As You May Never See Us Again
....Joel Craig and Sharlene Baker

Additional Information and Amendments to the North Carolina Troops 1861 – 1865 Volume I & II
....Charles E. Purser

Memoir of Nathaniel Macon of North Carolina
.... Weldon N. Edwards

General Robert E. Lee, The South's Peerless Soldier and Leader
....Captain Samuel A. Ashe

A Confederate Catechism
.... Lyon Gardiner Tyler

A Southern View of the Invasion of the Southern States
.... Captain Samuel A. Ashe

Life of Nathaniel Macon
.... William E. Dodd

Sherman's Rascals
.... Frank B. Powell, III

General Lee and Santa Claus
.... Mrs. Louise Clack

Prayers and Other Devotions for the Use of the Soldiers of the Army of the Confederate States
.... Female Bible, Prayer-Book and Tract Society

The Land We Love: The South And Its Heritage
.... Dr. Boyd Cathey

More information available at www.scuppernongpress.com
The Scuppernong Press
PO Box 1724, Wake Forest, NC 27588

www.ingramcontent.com/pod-product-compliance
Lightning Source LLC
Chambersburg PA
CBHW052205110526
44591CB00012B/2085